Anonymous

The Terrible Tragedy at Washington

Assassination of President Lincoln - Last hours and death-bed scenes of

the President

Anonymous

The Terrible Tragedy at Washington
Assassination of President Lincoln - Last hours and death-bed scenes of the President

ISBN/EAN: 9783337849948

Printed in Europe, USA, Canada, Australia, Japan

Cover: Foto ©Andreas Hilbeck / pixelio.de

More available books at **www.hansebooks.com**

THE TERRIBLE TRAGEDY AT WASHINGTON.

ASSASSINATION OF PRESIDENT LINCOLN.

LAST HOURS AND DEATH-BED SCENES OF THE PRESIDENT.

A FULL AND GRAPHIC ACCOUNT, FROM RELIABLE AUTHORITY,

OF THIS

GREAT NATIONAL CALAMITY.

ATTEMPT OF THE CONSPIRATORS TO MURDER

SECRETARY SEWARD, VICE-PRESIDENT JOHNSON, AND THE WHOLE CABINET.

A BIOGRAPHICAL SKETCH, WITH

A CORRECT LIKENESS

OF ALL THE PARTIES

IN ANY WAY CONNECTED WITH THE LAMENTABLE EVENT.

TO WHICH IS ADDED

AN AUTHENTIC HISTORY OF ASSASSINS AND THE DISTIN-
GUISHED PERSONAGES OF THE WORLD WHO
HAVE FALLEN BY THEIR HANDS.

PHILADELPHIA:
PUBLISHED BY BARCLAY & CO.
602 ARCH STREET.

Diagram showing the location of Ford's Theatre.

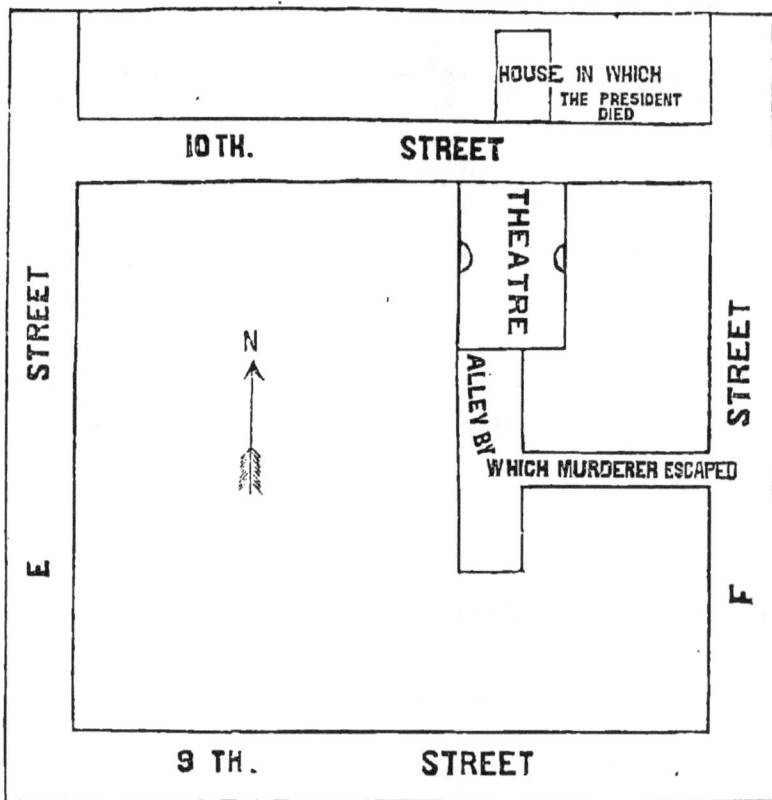

HOUSE IN WHICH THE PRESIDENT DIED

10TH. STREET

THEATRE

STREET

STREET

N

ALLEY BY WHICH MURDERER ESCAPED

E

F

9TH. STREET

Entered according to Act of Congress, in the year 1865, by
BARCLAY & CO.,
In the Clerk's Office of the District Court of the United States, in and for the Eastern District of Pennsylvania.

THE TERRIBLE TRAGEDY AT WASHINGTON.

ASSASSINATION OF PRESIDENT LINCOLN.

THE ASSASSINATION OF THE PRESIDENT.—A CAREFULLY PLANNED CONSPIRACY.

A CRIME was perpetrated in Washington on Friday night, April 14th, 1865, that will startle not only the people of the United States, but the whole civilized world. The President of the United States, sitting with his wife in a box in one of the Washington Theatres, was shot by an assassin, who, by the only exclamation he appears to have uttered, must be one of the secessionists whom the President has been most earnestly endeavoring to protect from the just retribution due to them for their agency in their wicked rebellion. During a pause in one of the scenes the assassin shot the President in the head, making a mortal wound, and then flourishing a drawn dagger, he exclaimed, " *Sic semper Tyrannis*,"* (the motto of the State of Virginia), rushed out of the back of the theatre, mounted a horse in waiting, and escaped. The crime appears not to have been the only one of the night, for a further despatch announces that an attempt was also made to assassinate the Secretary of State. At first blush, this murderous business would appear to be the work of a madman, but the particulars of the fearful outrage perpetrated on the President, and the simultaneous attack on Mr. Seward, show it to have been a carefully planned conspiracy, in which a number of murderous confederates must have been concerned.

This will be startling and terrible news to the country now in the midst of its rejoicings over the near prospect of peace, and ranging itself under the lead of Mr. Lincoln upon the side of mercy, forbearance and pardon towards those whose murderous partisans have struck him his death-blow. Nothing short of the interposition of Providence working upon the hearts of the people will be able to avert the instinctive impulse of the nation to punish this crime by some signal act of retribution that it sickens the heart to contemplate.

It is impossible to give a rational motive to the villains concerned in the murderous plot. Of all men in the United States, the traitors and rebels who have been in arms for four years in their effort to destroy the Republic, owe most to the kindness of heart, the conscientious endeavor to be just, and the resolute purpose to restore the fraternal relations of the people of the two sections of the country which actuated Mr. Lincoln from the day of his first inauguration to his dying hour. In every stage of the war which they brought on by their unhal-

* Thus be it with all tyrants.

(21)

lowed plots, he has been their powerful friend, protecting them at all times from those men in his own party who recommended, from the start, that they should be dealt with according to the severest dictates of stern and relentless justice. At any time since 1861, had almost any other Republican than Abraham Lincoln been invested with his power and beset with the appeals that were made to him for retributive justice upon the men who have wantonly and wickedly drenched the land in blood, many a traitor, now living as securely as if his great crime had never been meditated, would have swung from the gallows, which has no office if not made for such as they. Even at the hour when his death-blow was struck, he was standing, like a minister of mercy, appealing to the country to sustain him in the universal pardon and oblivion in which he desired to sink their crimes. And yet the fiends in the form of men whom he was thus guarding from punishment, struck him down! What depth of damnation is there deep enough for devils such as these?

We do not pause at this late hour to enlarge upon the terrible calamity to the nation, involved in Mr. Lincoln's death, in the crisis through which the country is now passing. We lose as sincere a patriot and as upright a magistrate as ever blessed the land. Even those who have been his bitterest foes will now admit this, for they have lost a friend who has stood by them in their direst need. He has borne himself ".clear in his great office," and may heaven send us one who will guide the country through its terrible trials as safely and as conscientiously as he made it the object of his life to do.

OFFICIAL GAZETTE.

Washington, April 15—1.30, A. M.—MAJOR-GENERAL DIX.—This evening, about 9.30 P. M., at Ford's Theatre, the President, while sitting in his private box with Mrs. Lincoln, Miss Harris, and Major Rathburn, was shot by an assassin, who suddenly entered the box and approached behind the President.

The assassin then leaped upon the stage, brandishing a large dagger or knife, and made his escape in the rear of the theatre.

The pistol ball entered the back of the President's head and penetrated nearly through the head. The wound is mortal. The President has been insensible ever since it was inflicted, and is now dying.

About the same hour, an assassin, whether the same or another, entered Mr. Seward's house, and, under pretence of having a prescription, was shown to the Secretary's sick chamber. The Secretary was in bed, a nurse and Miss Seward with him. The assassin immediately rushed to the bed, inflicted one or two stabs on the throat, and two on the face. It is hoped the wounds may not be mortal. My apprehension is that they will prove fatal.

The noise alarmed Mr. Frederick Seward, who was in an adjoining room, and hastened to the door of his father's room, where he met the assassin, who inflicted upon him one or more dangerous wounds. The recovery of Frederick Seward is doubtful.

It is not probable that the President will live through the night.

Gen. Grant and wife were advertised to be at the theatre this evening, but he started to Burlington at 6 o'clock, P. M. At a cabinet meeting, at which General Grant was present, to-day, the subject of the state of the country and the prospects of a speedy peace were discussed.

The President was very cheerful and hopeful. He spoke very kindly of General Lee and others of the confederacy, and the establishment of the government of Virginia.

All the members of the cabinet, except Mr. Seward, are now in attendance upon the President. I have seen Mr. Seward, but he and Frederick were both unconscious. EDWIN M. STANTON, Secretary of War.

THE PRESIDENT'S CONDITION.

Washington, April 15, 2.30 A. M.—The President is still alive, but is growing weaker. The ball is lodged in his brain, three inches from where it entered the skull. He remains insensible and his condition is utterly hopeless. The Vice-President has been to see him, but all company except the Cabinet, his family, and a few friends, are rigidly excluded.

Large crowds still continue in the street as near to the house as the line of guards will allow.

SECOND OFFICIAL GAZETTE.

Washington April 15, 3 A. M.—MAJOR-GENERAL DIX, NEW YORK.—The President still breathes, but is quite insensible, as he has been ever since he was shot. He evidently did not see the person who shot him, but was looking on the stage, as he was approached behind.

Mr. Seward has rallied, and it is hoped may live. Frederick Seward's condition is very critical. The attendant who was present was stabbed through the lungs, and is not expected to live. The wounds of Major Seward are not serious.

Investigation strongly indicates J. Wilkes Booth as the assassin of the President. Whether it was the same or a different person that attempted to murder Mr. Seward remains in doubt.

Chief Justice Carter is engaged in taking the evidence. Every exertion has been made to prevent the escape of the murderer. His horse has been found in the road near Washington. EDWIN M. STANTON, Secretary of War.

·THE ASSASSINS. ·

THIRD OFFICIAL GAZETTE.

Washington April 15, 4.10, A. M.—MAJOR-GENERAL DIX, NEW YORK. The President continues insensible and is sinking.

Secretary Seward remains without change.

Frederick Seward's skull is fractured in two places, besides a severe cut upon the head. The attendant is still alive but hopeless. Major Seward's wounds are are not dangerous.

It is now ascertained, with reasonable certainty, that two assassins were engaged in the horrible crime, J. Wilkes Booth .being the one that shot the President. The other is a companion of his, whose name is not known.

It appears from a letter found in Booth's trunk, that the murder was planned before the 4th of March, but fell through then because the accomplice backed out until "Richmond could be heard from."

Booth and his accomplice were at the livery stable at six o'clock last evening, and left there about ten o'clock, or shortly before that hour. It would seem that for several days they have been seeking their chance, but for some unknown reason it was not carried into effect until last night. One of them has evidently made his way to Baltimore; the other has not yet been traced.

EDWIN M. STANTON Secretary of War.

OUR SPECIAL CORRESPONDENT'S ACCOUNT.

Washington, April 14.—The city is full of the wildest excitement. President Lincoln, attended by his wife, was at Ford's Theatre this evening. About half-past ten, while the performance was going on, a man who had been seen standing near the door of the President's private box, entered it, and shot the President in the head. The ball entered the eye and came out back of his head. Immediately upon firing the assassin jumped from the box on to the stage of the theatre; as he jumped he held a long dirk in his hand and shouted "Sic semper Tyrannis." As the assassin struck the stage he missed his footing and fell into the orchestra, but quickly recovering his feet he jumped upon the stage, and brandishing his dirk ran behind the scenes and made safe his escape into a back alley of the theatre, where his horse was in readiness for him. Mounting his horse, he rode rapidly away, no one as yet knows whither. No pen can describe the excitement of the moment. The whole audience was petrified with horror, and not until the assassin had disappeared behind the scenes did men regain their senses. In an instant hundreds rushed upon the stage, crying for vengeance on the villain, but he had escaped. The President, upon being shot, told his wife he was dying and bade her good-by. He was quickly removed from the theatre by his friends, and taken to a house opposite, where a more critical examination was made of his wound by the surgeons, who pronounced it very dangerous, but possibly not mortal. Mrs. Lincoln, in great agony, accompanied her husband and remained with him during these trying moments. As the sad news spread over the city thousands rushed for the scene of the tragedy, and the house was literally besieged by most anxious inquirers after President Lincoln's injuries. As the moments passed by the question was repeatedly asked, "Is President Lincoln dead?" "No," was the reply, "but there is no hope of his recovery." At about a quarter of twelve the physician in attendance announced from the steps of the house, that the President was dead. Slowly the crowd began to disperse, and the sorrowful news passed from lip to lip. Various opinions are entertained as to who is the assassin. Suspicions rest upon a certain actor, who was seen in the theatre near the President's box just before the shot was fired, but in the excitement of the moment I prefer to mention no name. The revolver and hat of the assassin were picked up on the stage, and may lead to the discovery of the murderer. About the same time the President was assassinated, a man entered the house of Secretary Seward, under the pretence of having an important prescription from his physician. Entering the Secretary's room unattended, he cut his throat from ear to ear. The Secretary's son, hearing the scuffle, rushed in, but was met by the villain, who cut him in the face, and in the arm, and rushing down-stairs made his escape; not before, however, he had met Major Seward,

MRS. LINCOLN.

second son of the Secretary, who attempted to arrest him, but was struck on the head with a billy, but not seriously injured.

At this late hour I am informed by the Secretary's physician that no arteries have been struck, and that the Secretary will recover.

General Grant fortunately left for the North this afternoon, and, doubtless by his absence, has escaped the machinations of conspirators.

Secretaries Stanton and Wells also escaped the plot, as well as the remaining members of the Cabinet.

These are the briefest details of this tragic night. One arrest was made in the theatre of a man who said he knew all about the plot, but as yet the assassins have not been arrested. It is believed that a deep conspiracy is on foot to assassinate the remaining leading members of the Government.

It is now 12.30, and the excitement has not abated in the least; crowds are everywhere and the whole city is in the streets.

ANOTHER ACCOUNT.

ASSASSINATION OF THE PRESIDENT OF THE UNITED STATES;

ATTEMPTED MURDER OF THE SECRETARY OF STATE.

NO HOPE FOR THE PRESIDENT'S LIFE.

ESCAPE OF THE ASSASSINS.

Washington, April 14.—The President of the United States was shot while attending at Ford's Theatre to-night. It is feared that the wounds are mortal.

THE PARTICULARS.

Washington, April 14.—President Lincoln and his wife, together with other friends, this evening visited Ford's Theatre for the purpose of witnessing the performance of the "American Cousin."

It was announced in the papers that General Grant would also be present, but that gentleman instead took the late train of cars for New Jersey.

The theatre was densely crowded, and everybody seem delighted with the scene before them.

During the third act, and while there was a temporary pause for one of the actors to enter, the sharp report of a pistol was heard, which merely attracted attention, but suggested nothing serious, until a man rushed to the front of the President's box waving a long dagger in his right hand, and exclaiming, *Sic semper Tyrannis*, and immediately leaped from the box which was of the second tier, to the stage beneath, and ran across to the opposite side, thus making his escape, amid the bewilderment of the audience, from the rear of the theatre and mounting a horse fled.

The screams of Mrs. Lincoln first disclosed the fact to the audience that the President had been shot, then all present rose to their feet, rushing towards the stage, many exclaiming, "Hang him! hang him!"

The excitement was one of the wildest possible description, and of course there was an abrupt termination of the theatrical performance.

There was a rush towards the presidential box, when cries were heard, "Stand back!" "Give him air!" "Has any one stimulants?" On a hasty examination it was found that the President had been shot through the head above and back of the temporal bone, and that some of the brain was oozing out.

He was removed to a private house opposite to the theatre, and the Surgeon General of the Army and other surgeons were sent for to attend to his condition.

On an examination of the private box, blood was discovered on the back of the cushioned rocking-chair on which the President had been sitting, also on the partition and on the floor. A common single-barrelled pocket-pistol was found on the carpet.

A military guard was placed in front of the private residence to which the President had been conveyed.

An immense crowd gathered in front of it, all deeply anxious to learn the condition of the President. It had been previously announced that the wound was mortal, but all hoped otherwise. The shock to the community was terrible.

At midnight the Cabinet, with Messrs. Summer, Colfax and Farnsworth, Judge Carter, Govenor Oglesby, Gen. Meigs, Col. Hay, and a few personal friends, with Surgeon-General Barnes and his medical associates, were around his bedside.

THE PRESIDENT IN A DYING CONDITION.

Midnight.—The President was in a state of *syncope*, totally insensible and breathing hardly, the blood oozing from the wound at the back of his head.

The Surgeons were exhausting every possible effort of medical skill, but all hope was gone.

The parting of his family with the dying President is too sad for description.

The President and Mrs. Lincoln did not start to the theatre till fifteen minutes after 8 o'clock. Speaker Colfax was at the White House at the time, and the President stated to him that he was going, although Mrs. Lincoln had not been well, because the papers had advertised that Gen. Grant and they were to be present, and as Gen. Grant had gone North, he did not wish the audience to be disappointed.

The President went with apparent reluctance, and urged Mr. Colfax to go with him; but that gentleman had made other engagements, and, with Mr. Ashmun, of Massachusetts, bade him good-bye.

ATTEMPED ASSASSINATION OF SECRETARY SEWARD.

When the excitement at the theatre was at its wildest height, reports were circulated that Secretary Seward had also been assassinated. On reaching this gentleman's residence a crowd and military guard were found at the door, and on entering it was ascertained that the reports were based upon truth; everybody there was so excited that scarcely an intelligible account could be gathered, but the facts are substantially as follows:

At ten o'clock P. M. a man rang the bell, and the call having been answered by a colored servant, he said he had come from Dr. Verdi, Secretary Seward's family physician, with a prescription, at the same time holding in his hand a small piece of folded paper, and saying in answer to a refusal, that he must see the Secretary, as he was entrusted with a particular direction concerning the medicine. He still insisted on going up, although repeatedly informed that no one could enter the chamber. The man pushed the servant aside and walked quickly to the Secretary's room, and was there met by Mr. Frederick W. Seward, of whom he demanded to see the Secretary, making the same representation which he did to the servant. What further passed in the way of colloquy is not known, but the man struck him in the head with a *billy*, severely injuring the skull and felling him almost senseless. The assassin then rushed into the chamber and attacked Major Seward, Paymaster in the United States Army, and Mr. Hansell, a Messenger of the State Department and two male nurses, disabling them all. He then rushed upon the Secretary, who was lying in bed in the same room, and inflicted three stabs in the neck, but severing, it is hoped, no arteries.

The assassin then rushed down-stairs, mounted his horse at the door and rode off before an alarm could be sounded, and in the same manner as the assassin of the President. It is believed the injuries of the Secretary are not fatal, nor those of the others, although both the Secretary and the Assistant Secretary are very seriously injured.

Secretary Stanton and Welles, and other prominent officers of the Government, called at Secretary Seward's house to inquire into his condition, and there hearing of the assassination of the President, proceeded to the house where he was lying, exhibiting, of course, intense anxiety and solicitude.

An immense crowd was gathered in front of the President's house, and a strong guard also stationed there, many persons evidently supposing that he would be brought to his home.

The entire city to-night presented a scene of wild excitement, accompanied by violent expressions of indignation and the profoundest sorrow   Many shed tears.

The military authorities have despatched patrols in every direction, in order, if possible, to arrest the assassin, while the Metropolitan Police are alike vigilant for the same purpose.

The attack, both at the theatre and at Secretary Seward's house, took place at about the same hour, (ten o'clock), thus showing a preconcerted plan to assassinate those gentlemen. Some evidence of the guilt of the party who attacked the President are in possession of the police.

Vice-President Johnson is in the city, and his hotel quarters are guarded by troops.

We learn that Gen. Grant received intelligence of this sad calamity soon after midnight, when at Walnut street wharf, on his way to Burlington, N. J.

THE PRESIDENT'S LAST HOURS.

Washington, April 15—11 A.M.—At twenty minutes past 7 o'clock the President breathed his last, closing his eyes as if falling to sleep, and his countenance assuming an expression of perfect serenity. There were no indications of pain, and it was not known that he was dead until the gradually decreasing respiration ceased altogether.

The Rev. D. A. Gurley of the New York Avenue Presbyterian Church, immediately on its being ascertained that life was extinct, knelt at the bedside, and offered an impressive prayer, which was responded to by all present.

Dr. Gurley then proceeded to the front parlor, where Mrs. Lincoln, Captain

Robert Lincoln, Mr. John Hay, the private secretary, and others, were waiting, where he again offered prayer for the consolation of the family.

The following minutes, taken by Dr. Abbott, show the condition of the President throughout the night:

11 P. M., pulse 44; 11.05 P. M., pulse 45, and growing weaker; 11.10 P. M., pulse 45; 11.15 P. M., pulse 42; 11.20 P. M., pulse 45, respiration 27 to 29; 11.25 P. M., pulse 42; 11.32 P. M., pulse 48 and full; 11.40 P. M., pulse 45; 11.55 P. M., pulse 45, respiration 22; 12.8 P. M., respiration 22; 12.15 P. M., respiration 21, ecchymosis both eyes; 12.30 P. M., pulse 54; 12.32 P. M., pulse 60; 12.35 P. M., pulse 66; 12.40 P. M., pulse 60, right eye much swollen and ecchymosis; 12.45 P. M., pulse 70, respiration 27; 12.55 P. M., pulse 80, struggling motion of arms; 1 A. M., pulse 86, respiration 30; 1.30 A. M., pulse 95, appearing easier; 1.45 A. M., pulse 86, very quiet; respiration irregular; Mrs. Lincoln present; 2.10 A. M., Mrs. Lincoln retired with Robert Lincoln to an adjoining room; 2.30 A. M., the President is very quiet; pulse 54; respiration 28; 2.52 A. M., pulse 48; respiration 30; 3 A. M., visited again by Mrs. Lincoln; 3.25 A. M., respiration 24, and regular; 3.35 A. M., prayer by the Rev. Dr. Gurley; 4 A. M., respiration 26, and regular; 4.15 A. M., pulse 60; respiration 25; 5.50 A. M., respiration 28, and regular sleeping; 6 A. M., pulse failing; respiration 28; 6.30 A. M., still failing and labored breathing; 7 A. M., symptoms of immediate dissolution; 7.22 A. M., death.

THE ASSASSINATION.

ITS SECRET HISTORY.

BOOTH'S ACTIONS PREVIOUS TO THE MURDER.

Washington, April 17.—Developments are being made hourly, showing that the plot to assassinate the President and Cabinet was planned long ago, and that the conspirators were only waiting for a favorable opportunity to carry out their designs.

That the Knights of the Golden Circle were the originators of the conspiracy there is no doubt, and it is also assured that the 4th of March was fixed for the commission of the deed.

The assassination of the President throws light upon much which had seemed strange in the conduct of Booth during the past winter, and there is good reason to believe that in murdering Mr. Lincoln he was complying with an obligation of the Order of which he was a member, and which obligation has fallen to him by lot.

During the last two months he had seemed to be completely absorbed in some project, which none of his friends could fathom. In the midst of associates he would frequently remain silent; or, if conversing, would talk in a pointless way, as if thinking of some great trouble.

On the 4th of March his conduct was particularly noticed as being unusually strange.

During the morning, his nervous actions attracted considerable attention among his acquaintances, from among whom he suddenly disappeared, and was not seen again until a friend found him standing on the embankment at the north wing of the capitol, near which spot the President would necessarily pass.

Booth was dressed in a slouch suit, with his pants tucked into the tops of his boots, and an old felt hat drawn over his face. His friend hailed him two or three times, receiving no reply, and finally went up where Booth was standing, when the latter for the first time manifested his recognition of the gentleman, his manner conveying an impression that he did not wish to be recognized.

As the President passed, he turned away with his friend as if disappointed by the absence of some one, and preserved throughout the day a moody silence.

On Friday last he was about the National Hotel as usual, and strolled up and down the Avenue several times. During one of the strolls he stopped at the Kirkwood House, and sent into Vice-President Johnson a card, upon which was written :—

"I do not wish to disturb you. Are you in?
"J. WILKES BOOTH."

A gentleman of Booth's acquaintance at this time met him in front of the Kirkwood House, and in the conversation which followed made some allusion to Booth's business, and in a jesting way asked, "What made him so gloomy? had he lost another thousand in oil?"

Booth replied that he had lost considerably by the freshet; that he had been hard at work that day, and was about to leave Washington never to return.

Just then a boy came out and said to Booth—"Yes, he is in his room."

Upon which the gentleman walked on, supposing Booth would enter the hotel.

About 7 o'clock, on Friday evening, he came down from his room at the National, and was spoken to by several concerning his paleness, which he said proceeded from indisposition. Just before leaving he asked the clerk if he was not going to Ford's theatre, and added, "*There will be some very fine acting there tonight!*"

Mr. Sessford, ticket agent at the theatre, noticed Booth as he passed in, and shortly after the latter entered the restaurant next the theatre and in a hurried manner called for "*Brandy! brandy! brandy!*" rapping at the same time on the bar.

Yesterday a great coat, stained with blood, and which had evidently been worn as an overcoat, was found near Fort Bunker Hill, just back of Glenwood Cemetery. In the pocket was a false moustache, a pair of riding gloves, and a slip of paper upon which was written :—"Mary C. Gardner, 419."

This is supposed to have been worn by the man who attacked Secretary Seward, although the weight of the evidence indicates that all the conspirators took the same route, that of the Navy Yard bridge.

This morning Detective Kelly and a detail of patrolmen of the Second Ward, by order of Judge Olin, proceeded to the house of Mollie Turner, corner of Thirteenth street and Ohio avenue, and arrested all the inmates, from the mistress to the cook—eight in all—and took them to the police headquarters, to be held as witnesses. This is the house where Booth spent much of his time. Ella Turner, the woman who attempted suicide, being his kept mistress.

Secretary Seward is doing well to-day, and the indications are highly favorable for the recovery of Frederick Seward, who has somewhat revived from his comatose state. The assassins are still at large.

JOHN SURRATT.

From the description given of his assailant by Mr. Seward, suspicion has been fastened upon a young man named John Surratt, whose residence is about ten miles south of Washington, on the Bryantown road. His father was well-known and esteemed up to the time of his sudden death from apoplexy, within a year past. He owned a large country store, and held the office of Postmaster at the time of his demise. Young Surratt is reported to have been an active sympathizer in the Rebel cause, though by no means a man of sufficient daring to have planned the deeds with which his name has been unhappily associated.

His connection with the transaction, if such he should be found to have had, even more than Booth's, is regarded as indicative of the existence of a secret and powerful organization. From the lower part of Maryland ever since the beginning of the war, a regular system of intercourse has been kept up across the Potomac, and there have been evidences, from time to time, going to show that the Maryland adherents to the Confederate cause were exceedingly well posted as to the state of affairs in Richmond and beyond.

There was, for a long while, a very efficiently worked underground railway system between the Rebel capital and the vicinity of Port Tobacco and Leonard-town, Maryland, and not only correspondence but light freight and passengers were transferred over the secret route. According to the letters found in Booth's trunk, at the National Hotel, his accomplice had once urged a postponement of the "mysterious business" until "Richmond could be heard from"—probably by the clandestine route alluded to—which, following on the statement of the Richmond journals, apropos of Beale's execution in New York harbor, together with the arguments previously advanced, demonstrates almost beyond the possibility of a doubt that Booth and Surratt, or whosoever the actor's confederate may have been, were the agents of a bloodthirsty gang at the late Rebel capital.

If the criminals were the men who rode over the Anacostia Bridge, on the night of the murder, they were probably going over familiar ground to some point on the Potomac, whence they expected to cross over into Virginia, and thence to Jeff. Davis' distant retreat, if practicable—or by hook or crook to join Moseby's yet unscattered force, this side of Richmond—all in accordance with previous arrangement.

Captain McGowan's Account of the Assassination.

The following statement of Captain Theodore McGowan, A. A. G. to Gen. Augur, may be implicitly relied on as a correct version of the assassination of Mr. Lincoln

Washington, D. C., April 14.—On the night of Friday, April 14th, 1865, in company with a friend, I went to Ford's Theatre. Arriving there just after the entrance of President Lincoln and the party accompanying him, my friend, Lieutenant Crawford and I, after viewing the presidential party from the opposite side of the dress circle, went to the right side, and took seats in the passage above the seats of the dress circle, and about five feet from the door of the box occupied by President Lincoln. During the performance the attendant of the President came out and took the chair nearest the door. I sat, and had been sitting about four feet to his left and rear for some time.

I remember that a man, whose face I do not distinctly recollect, passed me and inquired of one sitting near who the President's messenger was, and learning, ex-

BOOTH ON THE STAGE OF FORD'S THEATRE, AS HE UTTERS THE MOTTO OF VIRGINIA.

hibited to him an envelope, apparently official, having a printed heading and superscribed in a bold hand, I could not read the address and did not try. I think now it was meant for Lieutenant-General Grant. That man went away.

Some time after I was disturbed in my seat by the approach of a man who desired to pass up on the aisle in which I was sitting. Giving him room by bending my chair forward he passed me, and stepped one step down upon the level below me. Standing there, he was almost in my line of sight, and I saw him while watching the play. He stood, as I remember, one step above the messenger, and remained perhaps one minute looking at the stage and orchestra below.

Then he drew a number of visiting cards from his pocket, from which, with some attention, he drew or selected one. These things I saw distinctly. I saw him stoop, and, I think, descend to the level with the messenger, and by his right side. He showed the card to the messenger, and as my attention was then more closely fixed upon the play, I do not know whether the card was carried in by the messenger, or his consent given to the entrance of the man who presented it.

I saw, a few moments after, the same man entering the door of the lobby, leading to the box and the door closing behind him. This was seen, because I could not fail from my position to observe it; the door side of the proscenium box and the stage were all within the direct and oblique lines of my sight. How long I watched the play after entering I do not know.

It was, perhaps, two or three minutes, possibly four. The house was perfectly still, the large audience listening to the dialogue between "Florence Trenchard" and "May Meredith," when the sharp report of a pistol rang through the house. It was apparently fired behind the scenes, on the right of the stage. Looking towards it and behind the presidential box, while it started all, it was evidently accepted by every one in the theatre as an introduction to some new passage, several of which had been interpolated in the early part of the play. A moment after, a man leaped from the front of the box directly down, nine feet, and on the stage, and ran rapidly across it, bare-headed, holding an unsheathed dagger in his right hand, the blade of which flashed brightly in the gas-light as he came within ten feet of the opposite rear exit. I did not see his face as he leaped or ran, but I am convinced that he was the man I saw enter. As he leaped he cried distinctly the motto of Virginia, "*Sic semper tyrannis*."

The hearing of this and the sight of the dagger explained fully to me the nature of the deed he had committed. In an instant he had disappeared behind the side-scene. Consternation seemed for a moment to rivet every one to his seat, the next moment confusion reigned supreme. I saw the features of the man distinctly before he entered the box, having surveyed him contemptuously before he entered, supposing him to be an ill-bred fellow who was pressing a selfish matter upon the President in his hours of leisure.

The assassin of the President is about five feet nine and a half inches high, black hair, and I think eyes of the same color. He did not turn his face more than quarter front, as artists term it. His face was smooth, as I remember, with the exception of a moustache of moderate size, but of this I am not positive. He was dressed in a black coat, approximating to a dress frock, dark pants, and wore a stiff-rimmed, flat-topped, round-crowned black hat, of felt, I think. He was a gentlemanly looking person, having no decided or obtruding mark. He seemed for a moment or two to survey the house with the deliberation of an *habitue* of the theatre.

2

FURTHER DETAILS OF THE ASSASSINATION.

PLOT TO MURDER THE ENTIRE CABINET.

Booth's Attempt to reach President Johnson.

STATEMENTS OF MISS LAURA·KEENE, MAJOR RATHBUN, AND CAPTAIN MACGOWAN.

SECRETARY SEWARD'S CONDITION.

ESCAPE OF THE MURDERERS!

LATEST FROM SECRETARY SEWARD.

He Receives the Intelligence of the Assassination of President Lincoln.

Washington, April 17.—The deep interest felt in Secretary Seward, has thronged his residence with visitors, among them several members of the Cabinet and Foreign Ministers.

He was informed yesterday, for the first time, of the assassination of the President, and of the attempted assassination of his son, the Assistant Secretary, and, to some extent, of the condition in which he then lay.

Though moved with the intensest sorrow and horror at a recital of the facts, his strength had so far returned as to enable him to bear up under the trying ordeal.

The Assassins—$30,000 Reward.

Washington, April 17.—Every effort that ingenuity, excited by fervor, can make, is being put forth by all the proper authorities to capture or trace the assassins of Mr. Lincoln and Mr. Seward.

The Common Council of this city have offered a reward of $20,000 for the arrest and conviction of the assassin. To this sum another of $10,000 is added by Colonel L. C. Baker, agent of the War Department, making the whole reward Thirty Thousand Dollars. To this announcement are added the following descriptions of the individuals accused:

Description of J. Wilkes Booth.

The description of John Wilkes Booth, who assassinated the President on the evening of April 14, 1865:—Height, 5 feet 8 inches; weight, 160 pounds; compactly built; hair jet black, inclined to curl, medium length, parted behind; eyes black and heavy; dark eye-brows; wears a large seal ring on the little finger; when talking, inclines his head forward and looks down.

Description of the person who attempted to assassinate the Hon. William H. Seward, Secretary of State:—

Height, 6 feet one inch; hair black, thick, full, and straight; no beard, nor appearance of beard; cheeks red in the jaws; face moderately full; 22 or 23 years of age.

Color of eyes not known, large eyes but not prominent; brows, not heavy but dark; face, not large but rather round; complexion healthy; nose straight and well-formed, medium sized.

His mouth was small, lips thin; upper lip protruded when he talked; chin pointed and prominent; head medium size; neck short and of medium size; hands soft and small, fingers tapering; shows no signs of hard labor.

He had broad shoulders, taper waist, straight figure—a strong looking man; manner not gentlemanly but vulgar.

He was clad in a dress overcoat, with side-pockets and one on the breast, with lappels; black pants of common stuff, new heavy boots; voice small and thin, inclined to tenor.

Number of Assassins Six.

The number of persons engaged in the assassination, as developed by evidence thus far educed, is six, including Booth.

Had each man engaged performed his part, the entire cabinet, with Vice-President Johnson, would have been assassinated.

Three Supposed Accomplices Arrested.

The town is full of rumors of the capture of Booth and Surrat; but an hour ago neither had been taken. Several arrests have been made—among them, three supposed accomplices of Booth in Prince George county, Maryland.

Frederick W. Seward Conscious.

Secretary Seward is doing well. Frederick is still in a dangerous condition, though there is hope of his life. For the first time he is conscious, replying to a question.

Pistol and Knife Found.

In the room above the one occupied by Vice-President Johnson, in the Kirkwood House, was found the pistol and knife which are of the same pattern as those in Secretary Seward's house.

INVESTIGATION—A CONSPIRACY TO ASSASSINATE EVERY MEMBER OF THE CABINET, ETC.

Washington, April 17.—The investigation in regard to the assassination is still progressing. A regular conspiracy to assassinate every member of the Cabinet, together with the Vice-President, has already been ascertained by developments which have just come to light. The names of the severally appointed assassins are, it is understood, known, and when all the facts are published the country will be astounded. We refrain from motives of public interest from mentioning any names.

The murderer Booth has undoubtedly made his escape into Rebeldom, as have also the other assassins. It may be sometime before he and the rest of them are apprehended, but they surely will be in the end.

Secretary Seward is regarded by his physicians as out of danger. Assistant Secretary F. W. Seward is also better to-day.

John Wilkes Booth.

This young man—for he is only thirty-three years of age—is the youngest son of the elder Booth, and is next in order of birth to his distinguished brother

Edwin. He was born on his father's farm near Baltimore, and is thus a Mary-lander. Like his two brothers, Edwin, and Junius Brutus, he inherited and early manifested a predilection for the stage, and is well known to theatre-goers and the public generally as a very fine-looking young man, but as an actor of more promise than performance.

He is best remembered perhaps, in "Richard," which he played closely after his father's conception of that character, and by his admirers was considered superior to the elder Booth. He was quite popular in the Western and Southern cities, and his last extended engagement was, we believe, in Chicago.

We have heard excellent actors say—and actors are not over apt to praise each other—that he had inherited some of the most brilliant qualities of his father's genius. But, of late, an apparently incurable bronchial affection has made almost every engagement a failure. The papers and critics have apologized for his "hoarseness," but it has long been known by his friends that he would be compelled to abandon the stage.

Last winter he played an engagement in the St. Charles Theatre, in New Orleans, under the disadvantage of his "hoarseness," and the engagement termi-nated sooner than was expected on that account. He had many old friends in that city, but this was his first appearance there since the inception of the rebel-lion. On his arrival he called upon the editor of one of the leading journals, and in the course of conversation warmly expressed his sympathy with secession. Indeed, he was well known as a secessionist, but he was not one of the "noisy kind." He has the same quiet, subdued, gentlemanly manner in his intercourse with others, that marks his whole family.

His last appearance in public in this city was on the evening of November 23, 1864, at Winter Garden, when the play of *Julius Cæsar* was given for the benefit of the Shaskespeare Monument Fund, with a cast including the three Booth brothers—Edwin as "Brutus," Junius as "Cassius," and John Wilkes as "Marc Antony." There was a very large and appreciative audience on that occasion.

If it is indeed true that he is the assassin of the President, the universal indig-nation which will consign him to lasting infamy will not prevent the expression of the profoundest sympathy and sorrow for those who are allied to him by blood; and whose condemnation of the act will not be less emphatic than our own; and all the more emphatic, because of their outspoken fidelity to the loyal cause, and their heartfelt admiration of the late President.

Mr. Edwin Booth.

Of course, no just-minded or thoughtful person would let the foul act of J. Wilkes Booth reflect upon the eminent tragedian Edwin Booth, his brother. But for the information of those who do not know Mr. Edwin Booth's opinions, and who may imagine that sentiments are inherited with family names, we will say that he has been a thorough Union man; he has on different occasions, here and elsewhere, for the benefit of the Sanitary Commission, and in many other ways, shown his sympathy with the Union cause. We are informed that political dif-ferences had caused a serious quarrel between Mr. Booth and his brother some time ago.

Frederick W. Seward.

Mr. Frederick William Seward, son of the Secretary, and himself Assistant Secretary of State, who was wounded by the assassin, was graduated at Union College, Schenectady, New York, in the class of 1849, and afterwards studied law in his father's office in Auburn and was admitted to the bar in 1852. A few years later he purchased an interest in and became one of the editors of the Albany *Evening Journal.* After the appointment of his father as Secretary of State, in 1861, he was placed in the position of the Assistant Secretaryship, and has discharged his duties with great ability and credit. * He was a young man of fine abilities, of most winning manners, and was endeared to a very large circle of private as well as political friends.

Clarence H. Seward.

It was reported this morning that Major Clarence H. Seward also was attacked by the assassin, but the statement is erroneous, as he was in New York on Saturday. He is a nephew, and we believe an adopted son, of Secretary Seward.

He was a graduate of Geneva, New York (now Hobart Free) College, was admitted to the bar, and has practised law in New York city. He volunteered in the early part of the war, and from a lieutenancy has lately been promoted to a majority in the volunteers.

Vice-President Johnson to have been also Assassinated.

It is very evident that the then Vice-President Johnson was included in the murderous programme of Friday night. On Thursday a man of genteel appearance took a room at Kirkwood's Hotel, where Mr. Johnson boards. For reasons best known to the proprietor or the detective, the name registered has not been disclosed.

During the following day he was particular in his inquiries about the room of Mr. Johnson, his whereabouts and habits. Since Friday night the strange lodger has not been seen; and on breaking open his room last night there were found concealed between the bed and mattress a bowie knife and navy revolver, and a bank book of J. Wilkes Booth, showing a balance of over four hundred dollars in bank.

During the afternoon of Friday, Booth called at Kirkwood's and sent to Mr. Johnson a card, as follows:

"Don't wish to disturb you. Are you at home?

"J. WILKES BOOTH."

When the assassination of Mr. Lincoln occurred, Senator Farwell, of Maine, was in the theatre, and hurried to Mr. Johnson's room and woke him up, to apprise him of the horrid tragedy. Upon entering the room he took the precaution to extinguish the light. It may be that this circumstance, or perhaps the early retiring of Mr. Johnson, saved him from assassination.

Major Rathbun's Statement.

The President's box at Ford's theatre is a double one, or what ordinarily constitutes two boxes, in the second tier, at the left of the stage. When occupied by the presidential party the separating partition is removed, and the two are thus thrown into one.

The box is entered from a narrow, dark hall-way, which in turn is separated from the dress circle by a small door. The examination of the premises discloses the fact that the assassin had fully and deliberately prepared and arranged them for his diabolical purpose previous to the assembling of the audience.

A piece of board one inch thick, six inches wide, and about three feet in length, served for a bar, one end being placed in an indentation excavated in the wall for the purpose, about four feet from the floor, and the other against the moulding of the door-panel, a few inches higher than the end in the wall, so that it would be impossible to jar it out of place by knocking on the door on the outside.

The demon having thus guarded against intrusion by any of the audience, next proceeded to prepare a means of observing the position of the parties inside the box. With a gimlet or small bit he bored a hole in the door panel, which he afterwards reamed out with his knife so as to leave it little larger than a buckshot on the inside, while it was sufficiently large on the outside in the dark entry for him to place his eye against with convenience and see the position occupied by the President and his friends. Both box doors were perforated in like manner. But there were spring locks on each of these doors, and it was barely possible that they might be fastened.

To provide against such an emergency, the screws which fasten the bolt-hasps to the wood had been partially withdrawn, and left so that, while they would hold the hasps to the wood, they would afford little or no resistance to a firm pressure upon the door from the outside.

Miss Laura Keene's Statement.

Prominent among those mentioned in connection with the incidents of the late tragical death of our worthy President, is the name of Miss Laura Keene, the actress. In order to place her right in the history, the following facts will suffice:

Miss Keene was behind the scenes at the precise time of the shooting, waiting to come on the stage. She was near the place theatrically known as the *tormentor*. She was on the northern side of the theatre, while the President's box was on the southern side.

Miss Keene's position was near the prompter's desk; but as that official was absent calling some of the actors, she placed herself near the point where she could more readily enter upon her part.

She was at the time expecting to see the ingress of Mr. Spear, whose part was at hand, and prepared herself to break his fall as he entered in a drunken scene: but instead of receiving Mr. Spear, Mr. Booth pushed his way suddenly through the side-scene, striking Miss Keene on the hand with his own in which he held the dagger.

She for a second looked at him, and saw it was another person from the one she expected—and instantaneously she heard the cry that the President was shot. The cry was spontaneous among the audience, and many of them were making for the stage.

She then knew something was occurring, as women were screaming, men hallooing, and children crying, as if a fire-panic had taken place. Miss Keene went to the front of the stage, and, addressing the bewildered audience, said—"For God's sake have presence of mind and keep your places, and all will be well."

Notwithstanding this appeal, the audience were boisterous; and while all seemed willing to detect the perpetrator of the great crime, but one made a move to this end. Scarcely had the perpetrator of the crime jumped from the President's box to the stage than he was followed by Mr. Stewart, one of the auditors.

As Mr. Booth crossed the stage he met and struck at the carpenter with the dagger he held, and instantaneously made his exit to the rear of the theatre, where his horse was in readiness, and thence made his escape.

Miss Keene, after momentarily arresting the panic and consternation in the audience, heard the cry of Miss Harris, saying, "Miss Keene, bring some water." Miss Keene, responding to the call, made her way, which was rather circuitous, through the dress-circle to the President's box, and got there a few moments after the occurrence.

There she saw Mrs. Lincoln, in the agony of a devoted wife, uttering the most piteous cries. Miss Keene attempted to pacify her, at the same time offering the good offices in her power, but she was convinced from her observation that human help was in vain. Miss Keene remained with the President until he was taken from the theatre.

FORMATION OF A REGULAR CONSPIRACY.

Washington, April 17.—The *"National Intelligencer"* says: We can state on the highest authority that it has been ascertained that there was a regular conspiracy to assassinate every member of the Cabinet, together with the Vice-President.

Booth sends up his Card to President Johnson.

Booth, it is said, sent his card up to the Vice-President at the hotel, but Mr Johnson could not conveniently see him.

A member of the Cabinet remarked on the day after the murder of Mr. Lincoln that the Rebels had lost their best friend; that Mr. Lincoln at every Cabinet meeting invariably counselled forbearance, kindness, and mercy towards these misguided men.

The *"Intelligencer"* also contains the following:

Harmony between Lincoln and Johnson.

We understand, from authority which we deem unquestionable, that a few days ago, after an interview between the late Chief Magistrate and the present one, Mr. Lincoln expressed himself gratified with their concurrent views, and he placed implicit confidence in the Vice-President.

THE OBSEQUIES.
FUNERAL CEREMONIES IN WASHINGTON.

Pilgrims from Every Quarter of the Union at the Capital.

APPEARANCE OF THE WHITE HOUSE.

THE SCENE IN THE EAST ROOM.

THE RELIGIOUS SERVICES OF THE DAY.

PRAYER OF BISHOP SIMPSON.
FUNERAL ORATION BY REV. DR. GURLEY.

A NATION'S SORROW OVER HER MARTYRED CHIEF.

WASHINGTON, April 19th, 1865.

To-day has been a bright, genial day for a sad, sad ceremony—the funeral of our murdered President. The first beams of sunlight came out with the booming of morning cannon, and as the day grew old they grew radiant till they were

almost of summer hotness. As I write I see away out over the roof-tops rejoicing
nature luxuriant in odorous blossoms and myriad budding leaves on the verdure-
clad Virginia hills. There is not a cloud in the whole sky. It seems as glad as if no
nation lay beneath mourning over its murdered dead, and paying him the last
honors the living can render to the departed; and yet so it is, for the spectacle
presented here to-day was but a part of the general sadness all over the land. The
whole city, ever since the death of the President, has been gloomy in crape,
stretching from house to house, as if to keep up the communion of sympathy and
the remembrance of our loss. Stores have been closed, business forgotten; for
the sole thought of the people has been the story of the dreadful murder and
condign justice on the assassin. Washington has been sad ever since Good
Friday, although a joyous time of the Christian year; but Wednesday, April 19th,
will ever be her grandest and her saddest day—grand because of the great out-
pouring, the extraordinary demonstrations of respect to the dead—sad because all
this love, all this honor, was for one who was gone—one who could no longer
thank them, or feel himself nerved to greater deeds of good to the people of the
whole nation—one who had been slain even by those to whom he was a friend and
benefactor.

Mourners from Abroad.

The announcement that the funeral would take place to-day drew together
immense numbers of people from every part of the country. Delegations came
from Illinois, New York, the New England States, Delaware, Pennsylvania, Philadelphia, indeed, every portion of the land, and numberless individuals came from
numberless different places. The Union League of your city, a deputation from
the Councils, and the members of the Perseverance Hose Co., were among the
arrivals, while from New York came the Union League, the different public
societies, and a number of such men as John Jacob Astor, Moses H. Grinnell,
Simeon Draper, and many others. Every train that arrived was full of men and
women clad in solemn black in respect to the memory of the nation's head. But
Tuesday night and Wednesday morning brought the largest numbers, and to them
were soon added thousands from Baltimore, Alexandria, and the different towns
and villages for miles around Washington. In the early morning, before the
great slumbering population had begun to appear in the streets, the city wore a
most funeral aspect, with its countless festoons of black flapping idly in the wind,
and its mourning flags stretching out lazily before the intermittent April gusts,
only to fall back suddenly to again hug the staffs that supported them. The
great dome of the Capitol stood out against the morning sky encircled with
badges of woe, and the White House was no longer white, but gloomy with the
trappings of death.

The Streets Filling.

The time for the commencement of the funeral services at the White House
was fixed at 12 o'clock; but before that time thousands began to pass towards the
Executive Mansion, clustering on Fifteenth street and Pennsylvania avenue, and
lining with a black, surging mass, the pavement and railing guarding the grounds
in front of the mansion. Soon the troops began to arrive and take their places in
the line of escort. Soon the whole avenue from Thirteenth down to Fifteenth
street was crowded with thousands who stood looking mournfully on the draped
mansion and all the sad surroundings, reminding them of their great loss and of
the awful crime which had been committed against them as a people. To this
motley *ensemble* of gleaming bayonets, uniforms of blue, and the monotonous
black of the popular dress, were soon added the innumerable carriages which were

to compose part of the funeral procession. The sun beat hotly down, and the eddying gusts 'shook up great clouds of dust, and sent them, with unswerving impartiality, over the whole throng; yet there was no dimunition of the crowd, but rather a constant increase of its numbers. The windows and porticoes of the Treasury and State Department were also filled with ladies, who looked down upon the scene before them with evident interest. Admittance to the White House could only be gained through the Treasury, and the doors were besieged from early morning by anxious ones, who were desirous of entering the house to witness and assist in the obsequies. There were people there who had travelled hundreds of miles to gain this request, and there were people who had not travelled at all; but all their pleadings were in vain. The most plausible stories, the most ingenious subterfuges, were resorted to, but all were useless. The implacable officials turned them off without mercy, compelling them to wander disconsolate, or be crushed in the swaying throng.

The Gathering in the Treasury.

Those who were fortunate enough to be gifted with the "open sesame" to the White House assembled in the west wing of the Treasury Department. A few minutes before eleven the doors were opened, and admittance gained to the Executive Mansion and the "East Room" over a long temporary wooden bridge, which spanned the galleries and uneven ground lying between the marble monetary palace and the boundaries of the presidential grounds. It required a long time for the many guests to pass, but the spacious rooms held all that were admitted. The arrangements, under the direction of Assistant Secretary of the Treasury Harrington, were of the completest kind, and every thing moved smoothly, without the slightest delay or confusion.

Appearance of the White House.

Passing over the long, wooden bridge bearded sentries stopped the guest at the gate until his ticket, entitling him to admittance, was shown. Then officers marshalled him through the entrance rooms to the East Room, where the body of the President lay in state. The exterior of the mansion was elaborately and tastefully draped. The pediments of white marble were festooned generously with crape, which wound in regular folds down the great, smooth pillars to the ground. The reception room was untouched. It was as always. But the light was dimmed to a funeral gloom, which made objects indistinct and shadowy, and prepared the mind of the visitor for the sad scene into which a few steps would usher him. When we entered it a distinguished company was assembled: committees in spotless black, with great white silk sashes passed across their breasts over their right shoulders; generals of both grades, admirals, commodores, congressmen, and citizens from every part, of position and influence. Members of the press were grouped together in silence over the long area. A sad group of soldiers, cavalry and infantry, without arms or accoutrements were massed on the right of the portico, their officers at their head, while scattered over the ground were other groups—all sad, all still, all impressed with the meaning of the occasion that had brought them together.

The East Room.

The scene in this room burst on one with a sudden pathos of woe, for every thing that could suggest it was present. The heavy curtains were drawn down over the windows, shutting out the sunlight, and long reaches of heavy crape mingled its sombreness with the gay gold of the brocade. The mirrors, eight in number, which in the times when the honored inmates of the presidential mansion were happy, reflected back in myriad tints bright scenes, scenes of joy, were now hidden in crape and barege. The ruddy yellow of the frames was hidden in black, and the brilliant polish of the pier glass lost its brilliance beneath the white disguise of fairy gauze. But it was not the gloom that saddened, nor the hangings that covered everything that looked of mortality, nor the abandonment of desolation in the city that smote the heart. There was something still more solemn, that spoke far more clearly of death, in the funeral catafalque and the silvered coffin that held all that was earthly of the great, the good, the true. It needed none of these raven plumes to tell of death, for there it was in all its ghastliness, under the gathering folds of the sumptuous canopy, covering the remains of Abraham Lincoln. It struck all with force. Not one among all who entered the East Room, no matter what he was—a total unbeliever or a fervent Christian—but felt that the King of Terrors was a mighty king, who spared no one in his anger, and sought his victims alike from the highest and the lowest.

The Scene in the East Room.

All that art can do, all that a desire for luxury can do, has been done to render the East Room beautiful. Even in its garb of woe the same beauty remained more lovely and even heightened by the grief that struggled with idle show, rendered the original beauty the more winsome. But on this occasion its natural beauty was heightened by an intellectual beauty. All the talent, the genius, the celebrity of our land were gathered within its comparatively narrow limits, and to their prestige were added all the mind and force represented in Washington by the Diplomatic Corps. The guests had been ranged in a great semi-circle around the catafalque. On the chord of the semi-circle was the corps of correspondents of the press of the country—gentlemen whose mission it is to criticise, instruct, and elevate the masses, who read their words with respect and profit. Between the great arc of distinguished men and the chord of chroniclers who make history was the catafalque, partially obscuring from the view of your correspondent the distinguished gentlemen who stood in the centre of the room, for the catafalque stood in about the centre.

The guests entered the room in the order of their arrival, without regard to rank. There were ambassadors, now congressmen, then members of the council of some grieving loyal city, which had already sacrificed hundreds or thousands of its loyal sons. A grave, gold-laced scion of the European aristocracy, and its many interests, was the arrival now, and after him came an humble, truly democratic representative of the municipality of Baltimore, modest in deportment, plain in dress, in manners, and in speech. Then would come a portly congressman, closely succeeded by some general with two stars, who had made a name amid the dangers of the battle field alike for his courage as a man and his devotion as a patriot. But there were few who were not distinguished in law, politics, war, or finance. To the common eye they were common men, with nothing to recommend them beyond their dress, but there was a purpose of countenance, an evidence of will and of power, that told the most superficial that these men presided over the destinies of nations and shaped the course of the civilized world. It was an interesting sight for the members of the press to study the great semi-circle that stretched around them. One of the most striking objects was a fine-looking man, who stood far above the ground, his outlines limned against a bareged mirror. He was wholly unconscious of the notice he attracted, but his dignity and manly bearing extorted admiration from every one—critic and unsophisticated. He stood there a statue—a living statue—with' health on his checks and a flowing beard that betokened his manhood, and many a man, enthusiastic on certain subjects even in the presence of death, suggested his portrait as a representative of the strength of our thrice blood-bought Union. But there were other interesting sights. In the throng before us was included the entire political intellect of the nation. The men who led us through the storms of war; the men who preside as monarchs in finance and furnished us the sinews whose strength hurled down the boasting rebel power; the men who, in the battle-field, unblenched by cannon roar or whistling musket-shot, directed the efforts of our gallant armies to the glorious ends of success; our great men; the men who in every trial and every defeat were proof against despair and equal to every emergency, were there, modest and unobtruding; but none the less meritorious to the curious eyes that sought for them. . Circled around the catafalque, rich in all that ingenuity could suggest, were these men, great in the field, great in the forum, great in the council hall. On the right of the corps of the press, in this distinguished gathering, were men most of them, perhaps, unknown to fame, but useful in their spheres, and all contributing to the strength and glory of the nation. The catafalque is easily described. Measurements are not necessary, for they bring no idea of extent to the reading mind.' It was a canopy of black arching over the remains of the murdered dead. He rested in quiet peace in a dais—a parallelogram which formed the base upon which rested the catafalque. A dais was reared for the better convenience of the sorrowing, who mounted it to take a last look at the dead, the martyred dead. To our right, as we have before intimated, were many of the most valuable men of our land—not distinguished in position, perhaps, but in their spheres invaluable.

We noticed among the myriad of faces that of Mayor Wallach, of Washington, and many of his Councilmen; the Mayor and Council of Alexandria, the city in which Ellsworth died; Messrs. O'Neill and Myers, Representatives from your State; Gen. Burnside, Gen. Hoffman, and Gen. Dyer. Their gaze was fixed on the black velvet coffin, richly besilvered by the nation, who bemoaned the loss of its honored occupant. Gen. Burnside was in citizen's dress, but his face was just the same as when he led our armies on the tented field, though tinged with the sadness of the hour. In the centre of the semicircle were the distinguished gentlemen of the Supreme Court and the Diplomatic Corps. There was a marked distinction, in dress at least, between these two great bodies. Belaced with gold, the ambassadors looked around on the gathering of distinguished men, with an air of calm indifference, although they could not look upon the dead without a pang of regret, and a respect, and a memoir of decided honor, of honor indeed while he was living. There was a great contrast between the Diplomatic Corps and our highest judicial body. One came out in all the tinsel and glory of royalty, which depends on ostentation for its safety, while our greatest court could not be distinguished from the mass of American citizens.

On the left of the Press Corps was perhaps the most noticeable gathering of all, for there stood the men who in the hour of our trial had delivered us out of defeat and crowned our sacrifices with victory. There was Admiral Porter—great, bluff old tar—the conqueror of Fort Fisher; and the conqueror, indeed, of the whole South Atlantic coast; there was Farragut, the invincible—he who opened the Mississippi to the Union armies; there was Shubrick; and last, though not least, there was Grant, the conqueror of the hitherto invincible army of Virginia—the man who by sheer genius and skill had driven the rebel cohorts from their chosen stronghold, and compelled them to surrender, in a friend's country, at the expense of the Confederacy for which they fought and died.

On the right there was nothing particularly noticeable, even though they were participants in the obsequies of the first-martyred President in our Republic. They were valuable men—all staunch men, but they played no great part in the drama of the nation's preservation. Those in the centre were, in their places, instrumental in the salvation of the Union, but their parts were secondary, for their weapons drew no blood. But on the extreme left, on the north side of the catafalque, were congregated the men who, on land and sea, had upheld the honor of the flag. Grant was there—the impersonation of modesty—quiet and unobtrusive among those who had contributed far less to the nation's success. Farragut, Shubrick, and other admirals were clustered around him, engaged sometimes in lively conversation—lively, we judge, from the smiles we saw at different times when something particularly pertinent had been uttered. Grant stood there a monarch among all—a plain, unpretending man, with close-shorn whiskers and a square, massive face—his three stars, denoting that he was the leading officer of the United States—the chief among its chief—were concealed, on one shoulder at least, by the great white silk sash which indicated his position as chief pallbearer. Sometimes he turned to the many major-generals grouped around him, and made some remark smilingly; but beyond the respect with which his every word was received, there was no evidence that he was the general-in-chief, after the President, of all the armies of the United States. There was no gorgeousness about him. The same style of uninterrupted rows of buttons, in clusters of three, marked his uniform, and the only means of recognition for those who had never seen him was the unmistakable face which had been reproduced in a thousand photographs.

The Funeral Ceremonies.

These ceremonies were conducted by Rev. Dr. Gurley, the pastor of the Presbyterian church, of which the dead President was a constant attendant. After the usual funeral services a prayer was offered by Right Rev. Bishop Simpson, replete with unction and religious patriotism, succeeded by a fervent prayer by Rev. Mr. Gray, of Washington. These services were read, these prayers delivered over a coffin strewed with camelias and evergreens, the offerings of the true-hearted and the sympathizing. The sermon of Dr. Gurley was a fine production, and all its prominent features are included in the condensed report, to be found in another page.

The Funeral Procession.

The sons of the President were present during the religious services, in company with many friends, including the wives and daughters of the prominent members of the government. Thaddeus, the younger one, seemed deeply affected, and bowed his head upon his hand during the whole of the ceremonies. His son Robert was in his full uniform of captain, and partook in the sorrow of his younger brother. Mrs. Lincoln was not present.

When the last prayer had been offered by Dr. Gurley, the coffin was removed by twelve sergeants of the invalid corps, and placed in a hearse, the like of which in grandeur has never been witnessed in Washington. So great was the size of the hearse that the coffin, though measuring six feet six inches in the clear, seemed as a child's when compared to the great capacity of the receptacle in which it was carried. When the coffin had been transferred, the procession marched on its way.

In the subjoined report we give some idea of its strength and magnificence.

Never before has Washington, or any other city, witnessed such a pageant, and in all human probability it never will again.

The Spectacle of the Funeral.

Eyes have not often witnessed such a sight as we witnessed from the lofty porticoes of the Treasury. We do not need to enter into its particulars, since a subjoined report covers many of its particulars. But the report can never express the newness, the beauty, even in the midst of grief, of this funeral. In the advance were the Veteran Reserves, men who had in battle proven their prowness. Following them were the marines, their celebrated band, the cavalry and the artillery. Pennsylvania avenue was not thronged, but packed with people. The roofs of the houses vied with the streets in the number of their occupants. The stream of men in blue and red, mounted and dismounted, were succeeded by the citizens in long files, extending the whole width of Pennsylvania avenue. It was a glorious sight, and at least thirty thousand men assisted in the grand proof that the Union is not dead in the hearts of the people. Never was a more splendid sight witnessed in Washington, never, perhaps, may it be again. The remains were at last deposited in the Rotunda of the Capitol, where they will remain to-night to receive the veneration of the people. They will leave here at 8 A. M. to-morrow, passing through Baltimore and Harrisburg to you city, arriving there perhaps at 8 A.M. on Saturday, where it is believed they will remain until 4 A. M. Monday, when they will pass through New York, Albany, and other cities, to the last resting-place in Springfield, Illinois.

THE PROCESSION.

At precisely two o'clock the line of march was taken up at the President's house in the following order:

10th Regiment Invalid Corps, with reversed arms, regimental flags draped in mourning.

Drum Corps of fifteen drums and ten fifes.

9th Regiment Invalid Corps, Colonel George W. Gile.

Marine Band.

Marine Corps, commanded by Major Graham.

1st U. S. Battery of Artillery.

84th U. S. Battery of Artillery.

(Numbering together eight pieces, 12 pounders, with caissons, etc., commanded by Brigadier-General Hall.)

16th New York Cavalry, Colonel N. B. Sweltzer.

8th Illinois Cavalry, Colonel Clendennin.

13th New York Mounted Band.

General Ketchem and staff.

General Slough, Military Governor of Alexandria, and staff.

Dismounted officers of Marine Corps, numbering about two hundred.

Officers of Navy and Army on foot, numbering six hundred.

Mounted officers of Army and Navy, numbering about one hundred.

Signal Corps officers. Field officers.

Marshal Lamon.

Reverend Clergy and Physicians in carriages, three abreast, and fifteen in number.

The drivers of these carriages had their hats trimmed with white cambric, and those who rode horseback in this part of the line wore white satin sashes across their bodies, the ends hanging gracefully down below their waists.

Hearse.

Bearing the mortal remains of the late Abraham Lincoln, drawn by six gray horses, each led by a groom.

The grooms were dressed in full black suits and white satin sashes, and had white cambric muslin tied around their dress hats, with long flowing ends. The ornamentation of the horses was quite simple, and consisted of black cloth rosettes, one of which was placed at the head of the horse, and another about the middle of the body, and were attached to the harness. The hearse itself was constructed with much skill and taste. In its simplicity it agreed with the character of the great man whose remains it bore, and in elegance it became the station of the Chief Magistrate of this Republic. It was ten feet in length, and about four and a half feet in width. The height of the platform on which the coffin rested was seven feet from the ground. This platform was supported by a pedestal-like parallelogram fourteen feet long and seven feet wide. A domed canopy surmounted the whole. At the top of the canopy was a gilt eagle covered with crape. The whole hearse was covered with black cloth relieved by layers of silk velvet. The seat was covered with hammer cloth, and on each end was a splendid black lamp. It was, altogether, fifteen feet high, and the coffin was so placed as to afford a full view to all spectators. The hearse was guarded on each side by a detachment of the 1st Virginia Artillery on foot.

After the hearse came the President's horse, with his saddle, bridle, boots, and stirrups. The horse was led by a groom.

Then followed the pall-bearers in carriages:

On the part of the Senate.

Mr. Foster, of Connecticut; Mr. Morgan, of New York; Mr. Johnson, of Maryland; Mr. Yates, of Illinois; Mr. Wade, of Ohio; Mr. Conness, of California.

On the part of the House.

Mr. Dawes, of Massachusetts; Mr. Coffroth, of Pennsylvania; Mr. Smith, of Kentucky; Mr. Colfax, of Indiana; Mr. Washburne, of Illinois.

Army.

Lieutenant-General U. S. Grant.
Major-General H. W. Halleck.
Brevet Brigadier-General W. A. Nichols.

Navy.

Vice-Admiral D. G. Farragut.
Rear-Admiral W. B. Shubrick.
Colonel Jacob Zeller, of the Marine Corps.

Civilians.

O. H. Browning, George Ashmun, Thomas Corwin, Simon Cameron.
The family, represented by Robert Lincoln and Thaddeus Lincoln, in a carriage.
The delegations of the States of Illinois and Kentucky, as mourners, in carriages.
President Andrew Johnson.
The Cabinet Ministers.
The Diplomatic Corps.

JOHN WILKES BOOTH, THE ASSASSIN OF PRESIDENT LINCOLN.

Chief Justice Chase and Associate Justices of the Supreme Court.
The Senate of the United States, preceded by its officers.
The House of Representatives of the United States, preceded by its officers.
Governors of the several States and Territories.
Legislatures of the several States and Territories.
The Federal Judiciary and the Judiciary of the several States and Territories.
The Assistant Secretaries of State, Treasury, War, Navy, and Interior, and the
Assistant Postmaster-Generals, and the Assistant Attorney-General.
Officers of the Smithsonian Institute.
(All of the above, after the hearse, were in carriages.)
Knights Templar and band.
City Councils of Philadelphia, dressed in full black, with black crape on hats,
with the words "City Councils of Philadelphia" in gilt letters thereupon.
The Members and Officers of the Sanitary and Christian Commissions.
Satterlee Hospital Band.
Perseverance Hose Company of Philadelphia, dressed in black, with the name of
the company on crape, in gilt letters, on high hats.
Washington City Councils.
4th U. S. Battery Band.
Ohio Delegation.
New Jersey Delegation.
California Delegation.
Treasury Band.
The heads of bureaus and the clerks in the respective offices of the Treasury
Department.
Heads of bureaus and clerks in the respective offices of the War Department.
Heads of bureaus and clerks in the respective offices of the Navy Department.
Heads of bureaus and clerks in the respective offices of the Interior Department.
Heads of bureaus and clerks in the respective offices of the Post Office
Department.
Offices and clerks in the Attorney-General's Office.
Offices in the Department of Agriculture.
Joint Committee of the Alderman and Common Council of New York.
The badge worn by the Committee was handsomely draped; the device being
the coat of arms of the city, having engraved thereon the respective names of
the members of the body. The badge was about two inches in circumference,
and appropriate in its appearance.
Surgeons mounted.
Surgeon-General Barnes and Staff.
Drum Corps.
Battalion from Quartermaster-General's office, known as the 21st Infantry.
Members of Councils of the City of Baltimore.
Officers of Custom House.
Quartermaster's Band.
Officers and Soldiers of the War of 1812.
Brass Band.
Capitol Circle No. 1, Fenian Brotherhood, numbering about five hundred.
Brass Band.
14th United States Infantry.
1st Regiment Meigs Home Guard.
2d Regiment Meigs Home Guard, Col. Tansell.

3

Employees of Quartermaster-General's Office.

Employees and operatives of the War Department.

Employees and operatives of the Navy Department.

8th Illinois Cavalry Band.

United States Military Railroad employees, numbering about one thousand.

Union League of Georgetown.

National Republican Union Association.

Delegation from Alexandria with covered wagon draped, and the motto, "Alexandria mourns the National Loss.

Alexandria Fire Department, numbering about two hundred, uniform red shirts, black pants, and felt hats.

Potomac Hose of Georgetown, D. C., numbering about one hundred; same uniform as Alexandria Firemen.

Mount Vernon Association; Soldiers from Hospitals.

Brass Band.

Mechanics and Workmen from Mount Claire.

Baltimore and Ohio Railroad Employees; Arsenal Employees.

Brass Band.

Massachusetts Delegation, in which General Butler walked.

Delegation from Philadelphia Union League.

Delegation from New York Union League.

East Baltimore Union League.

Sigel Union League of Baltimore.

Medical College of Georgetown.

Officers and Students of Gonzaga College.

Merritt Band.

Hebrew Congregation.

Brass Band.

Baltimore City Cornet Band.

Turners' Society.

Ancient Order of Good Fellows; Germania Lodge of Odd Fellows.

Carver Hospital Band.

Good Samaritan Lodge, No. 1, Sons of Temperance; Equal Division, No. 3, S. of T.; Aurora Division No. 9, S. of T.; Lincoln Division, S. of T.; Central Division, No. 12, S. of T.

Brass Band.

Empire Division, No. 18.

Hope Division.

Italian Societies.

Brotherhood of the Union; Bookbinder's Society; Typographical Society

Jewish Congregation.

Emery Hospital Band.

Colored Societies.

Benevolent Association of Colored People.

Harmony Lodge, No. 18, G. U. O. of O. F.

Colored Men.

King Hezekiah's Pasture, No. 3.

Union Grand Lodge.

The Funeral March.

The grand and beautiful funeral march, performed for the first time yesterday, by the United States Marine Band, was composed and dedicated to the occasion by Brevet Major-General J. G. Barnard.

The procession passed from the President's house down Fourteenth street to Pennsylvania avenue, and along the avenue to the Capitol buildings, where the remains of President Lincoln were laid in state in the rotunda of the Capitol.

All the soldiers in the procession marched about twenty-five abreast. Many of the civic societies marched fifty abreast, stretching entirely across Pennsylvania avenue.

Washington, April 19.—Early to-day the streets were crowded with persons, thousands of them from distant cities and other localities. Nearly the entire population was abroad. By ten o'clock every prominent point on the line of procession was occupied by those who desired to obtain the best view of the solemn and truly impressive pageant. In the immediate neighborhood of the Executive Mansion a dense and unprecedently large crowd had assembled. During the forenoon various bodies had met at the Treasury Department, separate rooms having been assigned them, and to these Assistant Secretary Harrington, who had charge of the arrangements, delivered tickets of admission to the Executive Mansion. They included the Assistant Secretary, the Assistant Postmaster-General, and the Assistant Attorney-General, Senators, and Representatives in Congress, Governors of the several States, the Judiciary, and others of prominence. None could enter the mansion without tickets, room having been provided for six hundred persons only, upon a raised platform, with steps on the east and north and south sides of the room. The corpse lay about the centre, the space being reserved all around the catafalque with chairs for the occupation of the immediate family of the deceased. It was here in the East Room that the bodies of Presidents Harrison and Taylor lay in state, but the arrangements on those occasions were far inferior to the present, for now artists had been employed, contributing of their skill and taste to produce the best possible effects. At eleven o'clock the guests began to arrive, a body of about sixty clergyman, from all parts of the country, being the first to enter. There was an interval of a few moments between the arrivals, and thus no confusion whatever was occasioned. The proper officers were in attendance to assign the guests to their appropriate places in the room. Heads of Government bureaus, Governors of States, members of municipal governments, prominent officers of the army and navy, the Diplomatic Corps in full costume, members of the Christian Commission, the Union League Committee of Philadelphia and New York, merchants of the principal cities, members of both Houses of Congress, and others.

There were honored representatives, holding the highest official stations, from all parts of our own country and from foreign lands, and under the circumstance of the assasination of a President, whose body lay before them, the scene was solemnly grand and impressive. At noon the President of the United States entered, in company with his Cabinet, all of them, excepting Secretary Seward. President Johnson approached the catafalque, and took a last but brief look at his illustrious predecessor, and then retired to a position immediately on the east and in full view of the coffined remains in his front.

At ten minutes past twelve, amid profound silence, Rev. Dr. Gurley, approaching the head of the catafalque, announced the order of the religious services, when Rev. Dr. Hall, Episcopalian, from the same point, read a portion of the Scriptures according to the form of that Church.

The opening prayer was made by Bishop Simpson, Methodist Episcopal, who in the course of it said that in the hands of God were the issues of life and death.

Our sins had called for his wrath to descend upon us as individuals and as a community. For the sake of our blessed Redeemer, forgiveness was asked for all our transgressions, and that all our iniquities may be washed away, while we bow under this sad bereavement which has caused a wide-spread gloom, not only in this circle, but over the entire land. An invocation was made that we might all submit to God's holy will. Thanks were returned for the gift of such a man as our heavenly Father had just taken from us, and for the many virtues which distinguished all his transactions; for the integrity, honesty, and transparency of character bestowed upon him, and for having given him counsellors to guide our nation through perils of unprecedented sorrow. He was permitted to live to behold the breaking of the clouds which overhung our national sky, and the disintegration of the rebellion. Going up to the mount he beheld the land of promise, with its beauty and happiness, and the glorious destiny reserved for us as a nation. Thanks were also returned that his arm was strengthened, and wisdom and firmness given to his heart to pen a declaration of emancipation, by which were broken the chains of millions of the human race. God be thanked the assassin who struck down the Chief Magistrate had not the hand to again bind the suffering and oppressed. The name of the beloved dead would ever be identified with all that is great and glorious with humanity on earth. God grant that all who stand here entrusted with the administration of public affairs may have the power, strength, and wisdom to complete the work of his servant so gloriously begun, and may the successor of the deceased President not bear the sword in vain. God grant that strength may be given to him, and to our military, to perfect victory, and to complete the contest now nearly closed. May the spirit of rebellion soon pass away. May the last vestige of slavery, which caused the rebellion, be driven from our land. God grant that the sun may shine on a free people, from the Atlantic to the Pacific, and from the Lakes to the Gulf. Not only safely lead us through the struggle, but give us peace with all nations of the earth. Give us hearts to deal justly with them, and give them hearts to deal justly with us, so that universal peace may reign on earth. We raise our hearts to thee, to plead thy blessing may descend on the family of the deceased. God bless the weeping widow, as in her broken-heartedness she bows under a sad stroke—more than she can bear. Encircle her in thine own arms. God be gracious with the children left behind him; endow his sons with wisdom from on high; prepare them for great usefulness; may they appreciate the patriotic example and virtues of their father, and walk in his footsteps. We pray thee, the bishop said, to make the assassination of personal profit to our hearts. While by the remains of the deceased, whom we have called a friend, do thou grant us grace and repentance of our sins, so that at the end of life we may be gathered where assassins are not found, and where sorrow and sickness never come, but all gather in peace and love around the Father's throne in glory. We pray thee that our republic may be made the stronger for this blow, while here we pledge ourselves to set our faces as a flint against every form of opposition which may rise up for its destruction, so that we, the children, may enjoy the blessed advantages of a government delivered from our fathers. He concluded by repeating the Lord's Prayer.

The Rev. Dr. Gurley then delivered a sermon, standing on the steps, and near the head of the coffin. He commenced by saying:

We recognize and adore the sovereignty of God. His throne is in the heavens, and his kingdom ruleth over all. It was a cruel hand, the dark hand of the assassin, that smote our honored, wise, and noble President, and filled the land with sorrow. But above this hand there is another which we must see and acknowledge. It is the chastening hand of a wise and faithful God; he gives us the bitter cup; we yield to the behest, and drink the draught.

This chastisement comes in a way heavy and mysteriously deep, at a time when the rebellion was passing away. The assassin has stricken down a man upon whom the people had learned to trust, and upon whom more than upon any other had centred their hopes for a restoration of the Union and a return of harmony. In the midst of our rejoicing we needed this stroke, this desecration, and therefore God has sent it. Our affliction has not come forth from the dust nor from the ground. Beyond the act of assassination, let us look to God, whose prerogative it is to bring light out of darkness and good out of evil.

He who has led us and well prospered us so wonderfully during the last four years of anxiety and conflict will not forsake us now. He may chasten, but not destroy; he may purify us in the furnace, but will not consume us. Let our principal anxiety now be that this new sorrow may be a sanctified sorrow, and induce us to give all we have to the cause of truth, justice, law, order, liberty, and good government, and pure and undefiled religion. Though weeping may endure for a night, joy cometh in the morning. Thank God, that in spite of this temporary darkness, the morning has begun to dawn, the morning of a brighter day than our country has ever before seen. That day will come, and the death of a hundred Presidents and Cabinets cannot prevent it. The people confided in the late lamented President with a firm and loving confidence, which no other man enjoyed since the days of Washington. He deserved it well, and deserved it all. He merited it by his character and by his acts, and by the whole tenor, and tone, and spirit of his life. He was wise, simple, and sincere, plain and honest, truthful and just, benevolent and kind. His perceptions were quick and clear, his judgment was calm and accurate, and his purposes were good and pure beyond a question; always and everywhere he aimed and endeavored to be right and to do right. His integrity was all-pervading, all-controlling, and incorruptible. He gave his personal consideration to all matters, whether great or small. How firmly and well he occupied his position, and met all its grave demands in seasons of trial and difficulty, is known to you all, to the country, and to the world. He comprehended all the enormity of treason, and rose to the full dignity of the occasion. He saw his duty as Chief Magistrate of a great and imperilled people, and leant on the arm of Him who giveth power to the faint and who increaseth strength.

Rev. Dr. Gurley, towards the close of his address, said:

I speak what I know and testify what I have often heard him say, when I affirm that that guidance and mercy were the prop on which he humbly and habitually leaned; that they were the best hope he had for himself and for his country. Hence, when he was leaving his home in Illinois and coming to this city to take his seat in the executive chair of a disturbed and troubled nation, he said to the old and tried friends who gathered tearfully around him and bade him farewell, "I leave you with this request—pray for me." They did pray for him, and millions of others prayed for him; nor did they pray in vain. Their prayers were heard, and the answer appears in all his subsequent history. It shines forth with heavenly radiance in the whole course and tenor of his administration, from its commencement to its close. God raised him up for a great and glorious mission, furnished him for his work, and aided him in its accomplishment. Nor was it merely by strength of mind, honesty of heart and feeling, and persistency of purpose that he furnished him. In addition to these things, he gave him credit for a calm and abiding confidence in the over-ruling Providence of God, and in the ultimate triumph of truth and righteousness through the power and the blessing of God. This confidence strengthened him in all his hours of anxiety and toil, and inspired him with calm and cheering hope, while others were inclining to despondency and gloom. Never shall I forget the emphasis and the deep emotion with which he said in this room, to a company of clergymen and others who called to pay their respects, in the darkest days of our civil conflict: "Gentlemen, my hope of success in this great and terrible struggle rests on that immutable foundation, the justice and goodness of God; and when events are very threatening and prospects very dark, I still hope that in some way which man cannot see, all will be well in the end, because our cause is just and God is on our side."

Such was his sublime and holy faith, and it was an anchor to his soul both sure and steadfast. It made him firm and strong, it emboldened him in the pathway of duty, however rugged and perilous it might be. It made him valiant for the right, for the cause of God and humanity, and it held him in steady, patient, and unswerving adherence to a policy of administration which he thought, and which we all now think, both God and humanity required him to adopt. We admired and loved him on many accounts, for strong and various reasons. We admired his childlike simplicity, his freedom from guile and deceit, his staunch and sterling integrity, his kind and forgiving temper, his industry and patience, his persistent self-sacrificing devotion to all the duties of his eminent position. From the least to the greatest, his readiness to hear and consider the cause of the poor and humble, the suffering, the oppressed; his charity towards those who questioned the correctness of his opinions and the wisdom of his policy; his wonderful skill in reconciling differences among the friends of the Union, leading them away from abstractions, and inducing them to work together and harmoniously for the common weal; his true and enlarged philanthropy, that knew no difference of color or race, but regarded all men as brethren, and endowed alike by their Creator with certain inalienable rights, amongst which are "life, liberty, and the pursuit of happiness;" his inflexibility of purpose that what freedom had gained in our terrible civil strife should never be lost, and that the end of the war should be the end of slavery, and, as a consequence, of rebellion; his readiness to spend and be spent for the attainment of such a triumph, the blessed fruits of which should be as wide-spreading as the earth, and as enduring as the sun—all these things commanded and fixed our admiration, and the admiration of the world, and stamped upon his character and life the unmistakable impress of greatness. But more sublime than any or all of these, more holy and influential, more beautiful and strong and sustaining, was his abiding confidence in God, and in the final triumph of truth and righteousness through him and for his sake. This was his noblest virtue, his grandest principle—the secret alike of his strength, his patience, and his success; and this, it seems to me, after being near him steadily and with him often for more than four years, is the principle by which, more than by any other, "he, being dead, yet speaketh." Yet, by his steady, enduring confidence in God, and in the complete ultimate success of the cause of God, which is the cause of humanity, more than in any other way, does he now speak to us and to the nation he loved and served so well. By this he speaks to his successor in office, and charges him to have faith in God. By this he speaks to the members of his Cabinet, the men with whom he counselled so often and was associated with so long, and he charges them to have faith in God. By this he speaks to all who occupy positions of influence and authority in these sad and troublous times, and charges all to have faith in God. By this he speaks to this great people as they sit in sackcloth to-day, and weep for him with a bitter wailing and refuse to be comforted; and he charges them to have faith in God; and by this he will speak through the ages and to all rulers and peoples in every land, and his message to them will be, "Cling to Liberty and Right; battle for them, bleed for them, die for them, if need be, and have confidence in God." Oh! that the voice of this testimony may sink down into our hearts to-day, and every day, and into the heart of the nation, and exert its appropriate influence upon our feelings, our faith, our patience, and our devotion to the cause, now dearer to us than ever before, because consecrated by the blood of its most conspicuous defender, its wisest and most fondly trusted friend. He is dead, but the God in whom he trusted lives, and he can guide and strengthen his successor as he guided and strengthened him. He is dead, but the memory of his virtues, of his voice and patriotic counsels and labors, of his calm and steady faith in God, lives, is precious, and will be a power for good in the country quite down to the end of time. He is dead, but the cause he so ardently loved, so ably, patiently, and faithfully represented and defended—not for himself only, not for us only, but for all people in all their generations, till time shall be no more. That cause survives his fall, and must survive it. The light of its brightening prospects flashes cheeringly to-day athwart the gloom occasioned by his death, and the language of God's united providences is telling us that though the friends of liberty die, liberty itself is immortal. There is no assassin strong enough and no weapon deadly enough to quench its inextinguishable life or arrest its onward march to the conquest and empire of the world. This is our confidence and this is our consolation, as we weep and mourn to-day. Though our beloved President is slain, our beloved country is saved, and so we sing of mercy as well as of judgment. Tears of gratitude mingle with those of sorrow, while there is also the dawning of a brighter, happier day upon our stricken and weary land. God be praised that our fallen chief lived long enough to see the day dawn and the day star of joy and peace arise upon the nation. He saw it, and he was glad.

Alas! alas! he only saw the dawn. When the sun has risen full orbed and glorious, and a happy, reunited people are rejoicing in its light, it will shine upon his grave; but that grave will be a precious and a consecrated spot. The friends of liberty and of the Union will repair to it in years and ages to come to pronounce the memory of its occupant blessed, and gather from his very ashes and from the rehearsal of his deeds and virtues fresh incentives to patriotism. They will then renew their vows of fidelity to their country and their God.

Rev. Dr. Gray, Baptist, closed the solemn services by delivering a prayer, concluding as follows:

God of the bereaved, comfort and sustain the mourning family; bless the new Chief Magistrate. O let the mantle of his predecessor fall upon him. Bless the Secretary of State, and his family; O God, if possible, according to thy will, spare their lives that they may render still important service to the country. Bless all the members of the cabinet; endow them with wisdom from above. Bless the commanders in our armies and navy, and all the brave defenders of the country. Give them continued success. Bless the ambassadors from foreign courts, and give us peace with the nations of the earth. O God! let treason, that has deluged our land with blood, and desolated our country, and bereaved our homes, and filled them with widows and orphans, which has at length culminated in the assassination of the nation's choosen ruler, God of justice and avenger of the nation's wrongs, let the work of treason cease, and let the guilty perpetrators of this horrible crime, be arrested and brought to justice. Oh! hear the cry and the prayer and the wail now rising from a nation's smitten and crushed heart, and deliver us from the power of our enemies, and send speedy peace into all our borders through Jesus Christ, our Lord. Amen.

The corpse was then removed to the hearse, which was in front of the door of the Executive Mansion, and at two o'clock the procession was formed. It took the line of Pennsylvania Avenue. The streets were kept clear of all incumbrance, but the sidewalks were densely lined with people from the White House to the Capitol, a distance of a mile and a half. House-tops, porticoes, the windows of every house, and all elevated points were occupied by interested spectators.

As the procession started, minute guns were fired near St. John's Church, the City Hall, and at the Capitol. The bells of all the churches in the city, and the various fire-engines, were tolled. First in the order of procession was a detachment of colored troops; then followed white regiments of infantry and bodies of artillery and cavalry; navy, marine, and army officers on foot; the pall bearers in carriages; next the hearse, drawn by six white horses, the coffin prominent to every beholder. The floor on which it rested was strewn with evergreens, and the coffin covered with white flowers. The Diplomatic Corps, members of Congress, Governors of States, delegations of various States, fire companies, civic associations, clerks of the various departments, and others, all in the order of the procession, together with many public and private carriages, all closing up with a large number of colored men. The body was conveyed to and deposited in the rotunda of the Capitol.

The nearest relation of the late President's family now here, are the two sons of the deceased, namely, Captain Robert and Thaddeus Lincoln; N. W. Edwards and C. M. Smith, of Springfield, Illinois, brothers-in-law of the late President, and Dr. Lyman Beecher Todd, of Lexington, Ky., Gen. T. B. S. Todd, of Dacotah, cousins of Mrs. Lincoln. Mrs. Lincoln was not present at the funeral; it is said that she has not even seen her husband's corpse since the morning of his decease.

Washington, April 19.—All the foreign ministers, with their attaches, in all fifty-six in number, were present at the funeral service at the Executive Mansion to-day. Their place in the procession was directly after the President and cabinet ministers. This for the first time in our history, was in accordance with the usage of foreign nations, where the Diplomatic Corps follow the monarch. Heretofore they have been placed in the programme after the ex-Presidents, the Justices of the Supreme Court, and members of Congress. Upon the arrival of the head of the procession at the east front of the Capitol to-day, the coffin having been borne to the centre of the rotunda, the President standing at the foot of the coffin, surrounded by a throng of Senators and high military officers, and a small number of Illinoians, as chief mourners, the entire company filling but a small portion of the entire place, Dr. Gurley, at the head of the coffin, uttered a few brief and impressive remarks, chiefly in the words of Scripture, consigning the dead ashes, once animated by the soul of Abraham Lincoln, to the course of nature, to return to its original dust. The deep tones of his voice reverberated from the vast walls and ceiling of the great rotunda, now first used for such a pageant, and during the impressive scene many were affected to tears.

THE NATION'S LOSS.
(*April* 15*th*, 1865.)

Oh woe! oh woe! oh woe!
What awful sudden blow
Has changed to funeral moans our songs of exultation!
But yesterday so bright,
To-day in darkest night
Are quenched the blazing lights of joy's illumination,
We stagger to and fro,
Ourselves struck by the blow,
Of this most vile, most foul, most fell assassination.
The truth to credit slow,
We ask: *Can* it be so?
Is he indeed laid low,
The ruler wise and firm, and faithful of this nation?

Oh grievous, grievous loss!
Oh heavy, heavy cross!
This orphaned nation's heart is tottering, reeling under!
From a smiling azure sky,
In the twinkling of an eye,
Down crashed the fearful bolt that cleft our Head asunder,
Alas! now shattered lies
That Head so calm and wise,
Alike for goodness famed, for strength and moderation;
With eyes that tears bedim,
With hearts full to the brim,
We lose, we mourn in him,
Alike with Washington, a Father of this Nation!

Oh horrid, horrid crime,
Bred in the foulest slime
Of Slavery's loathsome pool, all rotting with stagnation!
Oh, dastard, dastard crime,
Unheard of in this clime,
Where men wage open *war*, but scorn *assassination.*
Oh senseless, senseless crime,
Committed at a time

Of reawakening hopes of peace and conciliation !
Alas ! what dost thou gain ?
In fury blind, insane,
The *mild* one thou hast slain,
A *sterner* now will reign,
And thou hast roused again
The slumbering thunderbolts of Wrath's retaliation.

But, nation deeply bowed,
Be all thy grief allowed,
Allowed be too thy wrath, thy righteous indignation !
But, like thy martyred chief,
Temper thy wrath and grief,
With noble self-control and generous moderation.
Be just ! give each his due,
Let those be slain who slew,
Be blood for blood, the fair and lawful reparation !
But, Justice satisfied,
Let Wisdom be thy guide,
Keep Mercy at thy side,
Finish thy sacred task, *our Union's restoration !*

Then from the firmament
Will he whom we lament,
Our nation's martyred saint,
Wearing a golden crown,
Benignantly look down,
And let his blessing rest for aye upon this nation.
EMMANUEL VITALIS SCHERB, *from Switzerland.*

THE PRESIDENT AND THE PAINTER.

As every thing connected with the personal history of our late murdered President has now acquired a thrilling interest with the public, we make no excuse for giving the following incident in his life :

I have been urged by several friends to send you the enclosed poem, written down by myself from Mr. Lincoln's lips, and although it may not be new to all of your readers, the events of the last week give it now a peculiar interest.

The circumstances under which this copy was written are these : I was with the President alone one evening, in his room, during the time I was painting my large picture at the White House, last year. He presently threw aside his pen and papers, and began to talk to me of Shakespeare. He sent little "Tad," his son, to the library to bring a copy of the plays, and then read to me several of his favorite passages, showing genuine appreciation of the great poet. Relapsing into a sadder strain, he laid the book aside, and, leaning back in his chair, said :

"There is a poem which has been a great favorite with me for years, which was first shown to me when a young man by a friend, and which I afterward saw and cut from a newspaper, and learned by heart. I would," he continued, "give a great deal to know who wrote it, but I have never been able to ascertain."

Then, half closing his eyes, he repeated to me the lines which I enclose to you. Greatly pleased and interested, I told him I would like, if ever an opportunity occurred, to write them down from his lips. He said he would sometime try to give them to me. A few days afterward he asked me to accompany him to the temporary studio of Mr. Swayne, the sculptor, who was making a bust of him at the Treasury Department. While he was sitting for the bust I was suddenly reminded of the poem, and said to him that *then* would be a good time to dictate it to me. He complied, and sitting upon some books at his feet, as nearly as I can remember, I wrote the lines down, one by one, from his lips.

With great regard, very truly yours,
F. B. CARPENTER.

Oh! why should the Spirit of Mortal be Proud?*

Oh, why should the spirit of mortal be proud?
Like a swift, fleeing meteor, a fast flying cloud,
A flash of the lightning, a break of the wave,
He passeth from life to his rest in the grave.

The leaves of the oak and the willow shall fade,
Be scattered around and together be laid;
And the young and the old, and the low and the high
Shall moulder to dust and together shall lie.

The infant a mother attended and loved;
The mother that infant's affection who proved;
The husband that mother and infant who blessed,
Each, all, are away to their dwellings of Rest.

The hand of the king that the sceptre hath borne;
The brow of the priest that the mitre hath worn;
The eye of the sage and the heart of the brave,
Are hidden and lost in the depths of the grave.

The peasant, whose lot was 'to sow and to reap;
The herdsman who climbed with his goats up the steep;
The beggar who wandered in search of his bread,
Have faded away like the grass that we tread.

So the multitude goes, like the flower or the weed
That withers away to let others succeed;
So the multitude comes, even those we behold,
To repeat every tale that has often been told.

For we are the same our fathers have been:
We see the same sights our fathers have seen—
We drink the same stream and view the same sun—
And run the same course our fathers have run.

The thoughts we are thinking our fathers would think;
From the death we are shrinking our fathers would shrink;
To the life we are clinging they also would cling:
But it speeds for us all, like a bird on the wing.

They loved, but the story we cannot unfold;
They scorned, but the heart of the haughty is cold;
They grieved, but no wail from their slumber will come;
They joyed, but the tongue of their gladness is dumb.

They died, aye! they died; we things that are now,
That walk on the turf that lies over their brow,
And make in their dwellings a transient abode,
Meet the things that they met on their pilgrimage road.

Yea! hope and despondency, pleasure and pain,
We mingle together in sunshine and rain;
And the smile and the tear, the song and the dirge,
Still follow each other, like surge upon surge.

'Tis the wink of an eye, 'tis the draught of a breath;
From the blossom of health to the paleness of death,
From the gilded saloon to the bier and the shroud—
Oh, why should the spirit of mortal be proud?

* [This poem is by Wm. Knox, a Scottish poet, who died in 1825. It is preserved in a collection entitled
Christian Ballads," edited by the late R. W. Griswold, D.D.—*Publisher*.]

LINCOLN MONUMENT AT FAIRMOUNT PARK..

The late President Lincoln has become immortal. Millions in future generations will revere his name. It will go to posterity with that of Washington, and, like it, become all the brighter as time progresses. Although it is not absolutely necessary tô erect a material monument to perpetuate the memory of President Lincoln any more than for Washington, yet such a memento would exhibit the respect entertained by the people of the present time for the great chief who has fallen. It is, therefore, suggested to the citizens of Philadelphia, that measures be adopted to have a monument erected at Fairmount Park in memory of Abraham Lincoln, the sixteenth President of the United States. The City Councils would be a proper body to give shape to the necessary proceedings The people would respond to any well-digested suggestion having in view the speedy erection of a grand towering monument to the most illustrious man of the age.

Independence Hall.

This time-honored place has been arranged for the reception of the remains of the deceased President Lincoln. It is dressed in solemn grandeur, inspiring a sacred awe to those who enter beneath its sombre shades. The old chandelier is entirely enveloped in deep folds of black, and from the centre of the shaft the long robes of material pend in graceful festoons—spring, so to speak, from a base line just above the windows. This forms a sort of tent-covering. The black drapery is continued upon the walls, covering every thing from view except the following : The likeness of Martha Washington, that of Wm. Penn, Gen. Jackson, Gen. La Fafayette, Gen. Harrison, and the beautiful painting representing Washington on horseback at the head of his army. The paintings are festooned with drapery, the whole being done in artistic style. , The pedestal containing the old bell is elaborately draped. , It is designed to place the head of the bier against or towards the pedestal, so that the motto on the bell will be near the head of the honored deceased, "Proclaim Liberty throughout the land and unto all the inhabitants thereof." Steps will be placed leading to the two front windows of the hall, so that two entrances will be afforded the citizens. They will make their exit through two windows, to the rear, on Independence Square. The parties so entering will pass in single file on both sides of the deceased. This arrangement will allow twice as many to pass in review of the body than if the old plan had been adhered to. Allowing one person each second to pass in review, would be equivalent to 7,200 per hour.

A Noble Sentiment.

We clip the following from the Philadelphia *Sunday Times* of Sunday :

"Our Nation's Loss.—If our columns do not contain the variety with which we usually strive to fill them, our readers must attribute it to the deadening influence of the terrible calamity of Friday night. With our feelings absorbed by the conflicting sentiments aroused by the unprecedented crime committed in Washington, we are unable to write upon general subjects. The grief that caused the suspension of business yesterday, is felt as much in editorial rooms as in counting-houses and offices, and the pen refuses to chronicle any thing disconnected with the bereavement of the nation.

Every loyal citizen feels as if a near relative had been lost, and many of those who never saw the President experience the same solemn regret as if he had been a familiar friend. In the sudden falling of this unexpected blow the country is stunned, and is as yet unable to realize the loss. Coming in the hour of so much rejoicing, when twenty millions of people were exulting in the overthrow of the strongest bulwark of the Rebellion, its severity is doubled. The religious festival of Easter is as much clouded by this catastrophe as the fasts of Passion Week were cheered by the news of our military successes.

"Again the hand of Providence strikes the balance; we gain, and we lose. In our weeping eyes the single loss outweighs a thousand such gains, and there is needed a greater exercise of religion and philosophy than can be controlled by the majority of men, to say that ' all is for the best.' In our hour of deepest need, the President was given to us by heaven, and on Good Friday, the Day of Sacrifice, the day on which our Redeemer suffered on the cross for our sins, he is required from us. Truly, ' the Lord gave and the Lord hath taken away.' "

ABRAHAM LINCOLN IN INDEPENDENCE HALL.

We reprint here the report of the speech of the late President Abraham Lincoln in Independence Hall, on February 22d, 1861, (Washington's birthday), when he was on his route to Washington for the purpose of his Inauguration. It was his first speech in Philadelphia, and the portions which we have italicised give evidence both that he looked forward to the probability of assassination, and that what he said or did, he was, God willing, "ready to die by."

I am filled with deep emotion at finding myself standing here in the place where were collected together the wisdom, the patriotism, the devotion to principle, from which sprung the institutions under which we live. You have kindly suggested to me, that in my hands is the task of restoring peace to our distracted country. I can say in return, sir, that all the political sentiments I entertain have been drawn, so far as I have been able to draw them, from the sentiments which originated, and were given to the world from this hall in which we stand. I have never had a feeling, politically, that did not spring from the sentiments embodied in the Declaration of Independence. I have often pondered over the dangers which were incurred by the men who assembled here, and adopted the Declaration of Independence. I have pondered over the toils that were endured by the officers and soldiers of the army who achieved that independence. I have often inquired of myself what great principle or idea it was that kept this Confederacy so long together. It was not the mere matter of the separation of the colonies from the mother land, but something in that Declaration giving liberty, not alone to the people of this country, but hope for the world for all future time. It was that which gave promise that in due time the weights should be lifted from the shoulders of all men, and that all should have an equal chance. This is the sentiment embodied in the Declaration of Independence.

How, my friends, can this country be saved upon that basis? If it can, I will consider myself one of the happiest men in the world if I can help to save it. If it can't be saved upon that principle it will be truly awful. *But if this country cannot be saved without giving up that principle, I was about to say I would rather be assassinated on this spot than to surrender it.*

Now, in my view of the present aspect of affairs, there is no need of bloodshed and war. There is no necessity for it. I am not in favor of such a course, and I may say in advance there will be no bloodshed unless it be forced upon the Government. The Government will not use force unless force is used against it. [Prolonged applause, and cries of "That's the proper sentiment."] My friends, this is a wholly unprepared speech. I did not expect to be called upon to say a word when I came here. I supposed I was merely to do something towards raising this flag. I may, therefore, have said something indiscreet. *But I have said nothing but what I am willing to live by, and, in the pleasure of Almighty God, die by.*"

We reproduce this report *verbatim*, the President himself having mentioned to our Reporter that it was the most faithful verbal interpretation in type of any of his speeches which had ever been made. We reproduce it, not on account of this, but with the simple impulse to lay before our fellow-citizens the first words ever uttered in public in this city by Abraham Lincoln—the more especially as they mark the idea which had so frequently obtruded itself upon his mind, that he might ultimately become the victim of sectional vengeance.

LETTER FROM "OCCASIONAL."

Washington, April 19, 1865.—It is precisely four years since the mob at Baltimore fired upon the Massachusetts volunteers on their way to the defence of Washington. How strange it is that the anniversaries of some of the brightest and some of the saddest events should have been greeted by a great victory or a great calamity! Lee fled before the triumphant legions of Meade on the Fourth of July. Grant captured Vicksburg on the same day. Lincoln fell on the anniversary of the evacuation of Fort Sumpter, and his honored corpse is borne to its resting place on the same day when, four years ago, the first Northern blood was shed by traitor hands. And yet more expressive still—and I name it not to be betrayed into irreverent comparisons—our good President, after all his acts of forgiveness of the enemies of his country, died at their hands on Good Friday, the day of the Crucifixion of the Son of God and the Saviour of man. And I firmly believe if Mr. Lincoln could have spoken after the fatal shot of the assassin had shattered his brain, he would have exclaimed of his murderer: "Father, forgive them, for they know not what they do." And why did they not know it? Because they were taking the life of their best friend—he who had pardoned so many of their associates; and who, only three evenings before, had spoken authoritative words of clemency and reconciliation.

And do we ever reflect, in the midst of our grief and wonder that such a deed should have stained this age of progress and refinement, that Abraham Lincoln could have died at no time when his surpassing excellence would have shone with so rare an effulgence? He passed from us as the land was echoing with songs of joy over the triumphs of liberty. He entered upon eternity as a pious people were thanking God that he had stricken our country's foe. How much better than if he had gone from us in the gloom of national despondency! Even as the summons came, there was a wondrous peace at his heart, and a felicitous sense of duty done. No monarch ever had such a funeral. Although not so elaborate and ornate as the pageant of the dead Eighth Henry, or the return of Napoleon to the soil of France after he had fretted and smouldered away in the rocky island of the sea, it was the proudest tribute ever paid to the memory of an American President. The suddenness and the manner of his death intensified the national sorrow, and called forth a burst of popular gratitude without a parallel. I wish I could describe the wondrous scene. It was a lovely day. The air was filled with the perfume and the harmonies of jocund spring. Crowds had come from all the States. The government was typified in Andrew Johnson; the army was represented by Grant and his staff; the navy by Farragut and his sea-lions; the judiciary by Chase and his associates; the Cabinet, the Congress, the departments, the freedmen, the released prisoners, the penitent rebels, the clergy, the professions—the People, the base of the mighty pyramid, the foundation of private rights and public safety. I leave to others the filling up of the picture. Let me borrow from an old-fashioned New-England poet, the beautiful wreath he wove for Washington, that I may lay it on the great flag that covers and canonizes all that is left of Abraham Lincoln:

> " Before the splendors of thy high renown
> How fade the glow-worm lustres of a crown;
> How sink, diminished, in that radiance lost,
> The glare of conquest, and of power the boast !
> Let Greece her Alexander's deeds proclaim,
> Or Cæsar's triumphs gild the Roman name;
> Stript of the dazzling glare around them cast,
> Shrinks at their crimes humanity aghast.
> With equal claim to honor's glorious meed,
> See Attila his course of havoc lead;
> O'er Asia's realm, in one vast ruin hurl'd,
> See furious Zinge's bloody flag unfurl'd.
> On base far different from the conqueror's claim
> Rests the unsullied column of *thy* fame—
> His, on the graves of millions proudly based,
> With blood cemented, and with tears defaced;
> Thine, on a nation's welfare fixed sublime;
> By Freedom strengthened, and revered by Time.
> He, as the comet, whose portentous light
> Spreads baleful splendor o'er the gloom of night,
> With dire amazement chills the startled breast,
> While storms, and earthquakes dread, its course attest ;
> And nature trembles, lest in chaos hurl'd
> Should sink the tottering fragment of the world;
> Thine like the sun, whose kind, propitious ray
> Opes the glad morn, and lights the fields of day,
> Dispels the wintry storm, the chilling rain,
> With rich abundance clothes the fertile plain,
> Gives all creation to rejoice around,
> And light and life extends o'er nature's utmost bound.
> Though shone thy life a model bright of praise,
> Not less the example bright thy death portrays ;
> When, plunged in deepest wo, around thy bed
> Each eye was fixed, despairing sunk each head,
> While nature struggled with extremest pain,
> And scarce could life's last lingering powers retain;
> In that dread moment, awfully serene,
> No trace of suffering marked thy placid mien ;
> No groan, no murmuring plaint escaped thy tongue;
> No longing shadows o'er thy brow were hung;
> But, calm in Christian hopes, undamp'd with fear,
> Thou sawest the high reward of virtue near,
> On that bright meed, in surest trust reposed,
> As thy firm hand thine eyes expiring closed,
> Pleased, to the will of Heaven resigned thy breath,
> And smiled as nature's struggles closed in death."

THE FUNERAL CORTEGE.

Washington, April 19.—This nineteenth day of April marks an epoch in our history. Four years ago to-day, Union soldiers coming to the defence of the National Capitol were murdered in the streets of Baltimore. To-day the funeral obsequies of ABRAHAM LINCOLN, who fell by an assassin's hand, have been performed. He has saved the nation, himself he could not save. The murderous spirit of the rebellion and of slavery culminated in the violent death of our greatest chieftain, and found a willing instrument in J. Wilkes Booth, to carry out the

MISS LAURA KEENE.

hellish designs of the bold, bad men who sought the life of the nation. The deed is consummated, but the Republic still lives.

The procession commenced to move from the Executive Mansion precisely at 2 o'clock P. M. in the exact order laid down in the programme. It is now 3¼ o'clock, and still they come. Washington has never witnessed any thing like what is passing here to-day. The day is glorious—clear, warm, and genial—and it would seem that all our people must be abroad. There is a great influx of strangers here from abroad, and all the immediate country round about has contributed largely to swell the multitude. From early morn, up to the present hour, Pennsylvania avenue, from the capitol to the White House, on either side, has been one compact throng of human beings. It is not too much to say that a hundred thousand people witnessed the imposing demonstrations of the day.

To describe accurately the incidents of the occasion would require more time than we now have at command, as this must soon go forward, or it will fail to reach its destination in season. It may suffice for the present to say that all passed off in order, and nothing occurred to mar the solemnities of the occasion.

We may remark that at the point where we stood, on the Avenue, when the car passed upon which rested all that is mortal of the great deceased, there was a spontaneous outburst of indignation, not loud, but deep, against the deep damnation of his taking off; and this was not all—tears, copious tears, were observed on many a face. The people feel their loss, and they will avenge it; in no violent way, but through the channels of the law outraged justice shall be vindicated. This day, as well as that upon which the good man fell, will long be remembered; indeed, it can never be forgotten.

The City Prior to the Funeral.

The day is beautiful and quite warm. The Avenue is filled with persons to witness the mournful funeral procession. Civic and military processions are passing to the appointed place of rendezvous. All business is entirely suspended, and the citizens have turned out *en masse* to pay the last sad respect to the memory of the late President LINCOLN. Every window, housetop, and available spot is filled with people, though it will be two hours before the funeral cortege will pass.

Rumor.

It is rumored on the streets this P. M. that Judge CAMPBELL and R. M. T. HUNTER have been arrested in Richmond, by order of President JOHNSON. The story lacks confirmation.

Another Arrest.

JOHN T. FORD, proprietor of Ford's Theatre, was arrested in Baltimore yesterday evening, and is now confined in the Old Capitol Prison.

The Burial Place of President Lincoln.

Washington, April 19.—Governor OGLESBY to-day received the following despatch:

Springfield, Ill., April 18, 1865.—A national monument fund is on foot, and a plot of ground, six acres in extent in the heart of the city, has been selected as the burial place of our late lamented President.

SHARON TYNDALE, Secretary of State.

4

The following "Dirge" upon the death of President Lincoln was published in the *Evening Bulletin*, upon the very day of the announcement of his death, Saturday last, and by next morning (Sabbath) was set to music and sung in very many of the church choirs of this city and neighboring towns. It has since been sung in Washington, New York, Boston, and other cities upon occasions of his funeral discourses.—*Publisher.*

DIRGE.

[BY RICHARD COE.]

Toll! toll! toll!
On every hand,
Ye bells throughout the land;
Washington's great compeer now lies,
With death-sealed eyes,
And pallid face upturned towards the skies!
Toll! toll! toll!
On every hand,
Ye bells throughout the land!
Toll! toll! toll!

Weep! weep! weep!
On every hand,
Ye patriots in the land;
Brave Lincoln's dead! Great God! and can it be?
Henceforth there's nothing in mortality
That's serious!" Help us to look to thee!'
Weep! weep! weep!
On every hand
Ye patriots in the land,
Weep! weep! weep!

Pray! pray! pray!
On every hand,
Ye Christians in the land;
No more his honest face will greet the sun—
His day is finished, and his labor done;
A crown of glory rests his brow upon!
Pray! pray! pray!
On every hand,
Ye Christians in the land,
Pray! pray! pray!

Overwhelming Evidence against the Assassin.

BOOTH'S LETTER TO J. S. CLARK, ESQ.

Deeply Interesting Particulars of the Assault on Mr. Seward—Fearful Magnitude of the Conspiracy—Seizure of the Conspirator G. A. Atzeroth in his bed—Booth's Mysterious Movements previous to the Assassination.

Justice on the Felon's Track.

Prompt upon the heels of the staggering assassination, the most rigid, active and exhaustive examinations and investigations were opened to identify the blood-stained fellows and visit them with the full measure of public retribution. It was at once discovered that the foul murder embraced a comprehensive network of conspirators, whose original purpose was to take the life of all the leading members of the government, both civil and military, and thus paralyze the nation and throw both society and government into hopeless confusion. Hundreds of detectives were at once despatched in all directions. Several arrests were speedily made and are still being made. Amid the widespread excitement and suspicions, a number of innocent parties were inevitably arrested, and upon examination discharged. Other innocent persons have been painfully involved by the alleged principal conspirator. Several of the leading assassins have been identified beyond a doubt, while new evidence is daily coming out identifying others with the great crime. The government is still pursuing its investigations, taking testimony, and pushing its inquiries in all possible directions, but by an express order of the Secretary of War, all the facts elicited are kept *sub rosa* until the whole plot is fully unravelled. Some, however, have leaked out, which we are at liberty to give, together with a mass of interesting incidents and circumstances connected with the tragedy, which have been accumulating with fairly oppressive profusion from the hour of the murder to the present moment.

John Wilkes Booth.

As to the most conspicuous actor in the startling drama, public opinion fastened at once with terrible tenacity upon John Wilkes Booth as the murderer of the President, and the evidence convicting him of the monstrous crime has since rolled up in massive proportions. Laura Keene, the actress, who was performing on the night of the tragedy, in the play entitled the American Cousin, identifies him positively. Nor is this lady alone in her identification. Another actor, Harry Hawk, whose father lives in Chicago, and who was also acting at Ford's theatre on the eventful night, wrote to his father soon after the tragedy, giving some interesting facts. We give that portion of the letter relating to the great calamity, as follows.

Letter from the "Asa Trenchard" of the Tragedy.

Washington, Sunday, April 16.—This is the first opportunity I have had to write to you since the assassination of our dear President, on Friday night, as I have been in custody nearly ever since. I was one of the principal witnesses of that sad affair, being the only one on the stage at the time of the fatal shot.

I was playing "Asa Trenchard" in the American Cousin. The "old lady" of the theatre had just gone off the stage, and I was answering her exit speech when I heard the shot fired. I turned, looked up at the President's box, heard the man exclaim "*Sic semper tyrannis,*" saw him jump from the box, seize the flag on the staff, and drop to the stage; he slipped when he gained the stage, but he got upon his feet in a moment, brandished a large knife, saying, "The South shall be free!" turned his face in the direction I stood, and I recognized him as John Wilkes Booth. He ran towards me, and I (seeing the knife, I thought I was the one he was after), ran off the stage and up a flight of stairs. He made his escape out of a door directly in the rear of the theatre, mounted a horse and rode off.

The above all occurred in the space of a quarter of a minute, and at the time I did not know that the President was shot—although, if I had tried to stop him he would have stabbed me.

I am now under one thousand dollars bail to appear as a witness when Booth is tried, if caught.

All the above I have sworn to. You may imagine the excitement in the theatre, which was crowded, with cries of "Hang him!" "Who was he?" etc. from every one present.

In·about fifteen minutes after the occurrence the President was carried out and across the street. I was requested to walk down to the police head-quarters and give my evidence. They then put me under one thousand dollars bond, to appear at ten o'clock next morning. I then walked about for some time as the city was wild with excitement, and then I went to bed. At half-past three I was called by an aid of the President, to go to the house where he was lying, Secretary Stanton and other high officials assembled there. I did so, and went to bed again. On Saturday I gave bail.

It was the saddest thing I ever knew. The city only the night before was illuminated, and everybody was so happy. Now it is all sadness. Everbody looks gloomy and sad.

On that night the play was going off so well, Mr. and Mrs. Lincoln enjoyed it so much. She was laughing at my speech when the shot was fired. In fact, it was one laugh from the time the curtain went up until it fell; and to think of such a sorrowful ending! It is an era in my life that I never shall forget. Inclosed is a piece of the fringe of the flag the President was holding when shot.

Startling Developments.

Further developments serve to confirm that the plot to assassinate the President and Cabinet was planned long ago, and that the conspirators were only waiting for a favorable opportunity to carry out their designs. That the "Knights of the Golden Circle" were the originators of the conspiracy there is no doubt, and it is also assumed that the 4th of March was fixed for the commission of the deed. The assassination of Mr. Lincoln throws light upon much which had seemed strange in the conduct of Booth during the past winter, and there is good reason to believe that in murdering Mr. Lincoln he was complying with an obligation of the order of which he was a member, and which obligation had fallen on him by lot.

Booth in Boston.

Boston, April 15th. John Wilkes Booth was in this city during the latter part of last week, and we believe as late as last Monday of this week.

He has frequently visited Boston, having friends here, and we did not hear that his visit on this occasion was in any way connected with business. He has appeared upon the stage only a few times this season, having interested himself in oil speculations, and by that means becoming quite wealthy.

At the beginning of the season he gave up all engagements that he had already made, and for some time devoted himself almost exclusively to his business at Oil Creek, where at one time, at least, he was associated with an old friend who formerly resided in the South.

His last appearance on the stage in this city was at the Howard Atheneum, about a year since. At that time he was vehement and bitter in denunciations of Mr. Lincoln and his administration, and so violent in his expressions of joy over every Union defeat, that he was frequently cautioned, and at last avoided by his brother actors.

When he left the city he expressed his undying hatred for the North and the Union, and threw out some vague hints for vengeance, which were not regarded at the time as meaning any more than that the rebellion should succeed.

Statement of an Eye-witness.

Mr. James P. Ferguson, who was present at Ford's on the night of the assassination, makes a statement to the following purport:

He went to the theatre with a lady on Friday night, for the express purpose of seeing General Grant, who was announced to be present. Mr. Ferguson saw the presidential party enter the box, but of course did not see the Lieutenant-General. He, however, continued to watch the box, thinking the General might intend to slip quietly in, in order to avoid the demonstrations that would attend his re-cognition.

When the second scene of the third act of the play was reached, Mr. Ferguson saw and recognized John Wilkes Booth making his way along the dress-circle to the President's box. Of this box Mr. Ferguson had an excellent view, being seated in the dress circle just opposite to it, next to the private boxes on the other side of the circle. This seat he had purposely chosen to afford his companion a good view of the Lieutenant-General, and, for the reason already stated, was narrowly watching the entrance to it.

Mr. Ferguson and Booth had met in the afternoon and conversed, and were well acquainted with each other, so that the former immediately recognized him. Booth stopped two steps from the door, took off his hat, and holding it in his left hand, leaned against the wall behind him. In this attitude he remained for half a minute, then, adds, Mr. Ferguson, he stepped down one step, put his hand on the door of the little corridor leading to the box, bent his knee against it. The door opened, and Booth entered, and was for the time hidden from Mr. Ferguson's sight.

Mr. Ferguson watched for his appearance in the box, desiring to see who in that party the actor could be on such intimate terms with, as to feel warranted in taking such a liberty. Whether Booth shut the door of the little corridor or left it open behind him, Mr. Ferguson fears to state positively; but from what he observed of the door, and for reasons hereafter to be stated, believes he did shut it. The shot was the next thing Mr. Ferguson remembers. He saw the smoke, then perceived Booth standing upright, with both hands raised, but at that moment saw no weapon or any thing else in either. Booth then sprang to the front of the box, laid his left hand on the railing in front, was checked an instant, evidently by his coat or pants being caught in something, or held back by some-body. (It was Major Rathbun.)

A post in front obstructed the view of Mr. Fergurson, but Booth soon changed his position, and was again clearly seen by Mr. F. He now had a knife in his right hand, which he also laid upon the railing, as he already had his left, and vaulted out. As his legs passed between the folds of the flags decorating the box, his spur, which he wore on the right heel, caught the drapery, and brought it down, tearing a strip with it. When he let go the railing, he still clutched the shining knife. He crouched as he fell, falling on one knee, and stretched forth both hands to help himself to recover an erect position, which he did with the rapidity and easy agility of an athletic.

Having recovered his equilibrium, Booth strode across the stage to the first entrance, passing behind the actor on the stage (Harry Hawk.) When he reached the other side of the stage, just ere he became invisible, by passing into the entrance, he looked up, and Mr. Ferguson said he heard him say, "I have done it," and then he lost sight of him.

Mr. Ferguson visited the theatre on the day following the murder, and, with Miss Harris, the lady who was in the box with the President, her father, Judge Olin, of the Criminal Court, and Judge Carter, examined the box.

The puzzling hole in the unused door of the box was closely scrutinized by the light of a candle, and was found to possess indubitable marks of *having been whittled with a knife.* The ball extracted from the head of the President is of much larger diameter than the hole. The edges' of the hole show the marks of a knife-blade very clearly.

When the shot had been fired, Miss Harris rose to her feet to call for water for Mr. Lincoln, and distinctly noticed a bar of wood placed across the door of the little corridor, one end resting against the wall into which it was partially let by a cut, or rather an indentation, scooped in the wall. The other end was braced against the opposite side of the door frame. This bar, as the door opens inward, would effectually delay, if not wholly prevent, all ingress into the box from the dress circle, and would also detain the egress of any one in the box.

Booth on Immortal Fame.

It is reported that the now notorious Booth remarked to a prominent citizen. of Cleveland a year and a half ago, that "the man who killed Abraham Lincoln would occupy a higher niche of fame than George Washington." During a the-atrical engagement of his at Chicago, in 1863, he remarked one day, "What a glorious opportunity there is for a man to immortalize himself by killing Lincoln." "What good would that do?" he was asked. He then quoted these lines :

> "The ambitious youth who fired the Ephesian dome
> Outlives in fame the pious fool who reared it."

"Well, who was that ambitious youth—what was his name?" was then asked "That I don't know," replied Booth. "Then where's the fame you speak of?" This, our informant tells us, nonplussed him. From this it would seem that the assassin has had the commission of this horrid crime in his mind for at least two or three years.

Remarkable Letter of the Assassin.

The following verbatim copy of a letter in writing, which is in the hand-writing of John Wilkes Booth, the murderer of Mr. Lincoln, has been furnished to the press by Hon. William Millward, U. S. Marshal of the Eastern District of Penn- sylvania. It was handed over to that officer by John S. Clarke, wno is a brother-in-law of Mr. Booth. The history connected with it is somewhat peculiar. In November, 1864, the paper was deposited with Mr. Clarke by Booth, in a sealed envelope, "for safe keeping," Mr. Clarke being ignorant of its contents. In January last Booth called at Mr. Clarke's house, asked for the package and it was given up to him. It is now supposed that at that time he took out the paper and added to it his signature, which appears to be in a different ink from that used in the body of the letter, and also from the language employed could not have been put to it originally. Afterwards he returned the package to Mr. Clarke again for safe keeping, sealed, and bearing the superscription "J. Wilkes Booth."

The inclosure was preserved by the family without suspicion of its nature. After the afflicting information of the assassination of the President, which came upon the family of Mr. Clarke with crushing force, it was considered proper to open the envelope. There were found in it the following paper, with some seven-thirty United States bonds, and certificates of shares in oil companies. Mr. Clark promptly handed over the paper to Marshal Millward, in whose custody it now remains. From a perusal of this paper it seems to have been prepared by Booth as a vindication of some desperate act which he had in contemplation ; and from the language used it is probable that it was a plot to abduct the President and carry him off to Virginia. If this was meditated it failed, and from making a prisoner of the President up to his assassination was an easy step for a man of perverted principles. The italics are Booth's own. The letter is as follows :

——, ——, 1864.

MY DEAR SIR : You may use this as you think best. But as some may wish to know *when, who* and *why*, and as I know not *how*, to direct, I give it (in the words of your master).

To Whom it May Concern :

Right or wrong, God judge me, not man. For be my motive good or bad, of one thing I am sure, the lasting condemnation of the North.

I love peace more than life. Have loved the Union beyond expression. For four years have I waited, hoped and prayed for the dark clouds to break, and for a restoration of our former sunshine. To wait longer would be a crime. All hope for peace is dead. My prayers have proved as idle as my hopes. God's will be done. I go to see and share the bitter end.

I have ever held the South were right. The very nomination of Abraham Lincoln, four years ago, spoke plainly, war—war upon Southern rights and institutions. His election proved it. " Await an overt act." Yes, till you are bound and plundered. What folly ! The South was wise. Who thinks of argument or patience when the finger of his enemy presses on the trigger ? In a *foreign war* I, too, could say, "country, right or wrong." But in a struggle *such as ours*, (where the brother tries to pierce the brother's heart), for God's sake, choose the right. When a country like this spurns *justice* from her side she forfeits the allegiance of every honest freeman, and should leave him, untrammelled by any fealty soever, to act as his conscience may approve.

People of the North ! to hate tyranny, to love liberty and justice, to strike at wrong and oppression, was the teaching of our fathers. The study of our early history will not let *me* forget it, and may it never.

This country was formed for the *white*, not for the black man. And looking upon *African slavery* from the same stand-point held by the noble framers of our Constitution, I, for one, have ever considered *it* one of the greatest blessings (for themselves and for us) that God ever bestowed upon a favored nation. Witness heretofore our wealth and power, witness their elevation and enlightenment above their race elsewhere. I have lived among it most of my life, and have seen *less* harsh treatment from master to man than I have beheld in the North from father to son. Yet, heaven knows, *no one* would be willing to do *more* for the negro race than I, could I but see a way to *still better their* condition.

But Lincoln's policy is only preparing the way for their total annihilation. The South *are not, nor have been fighting* for the continuance of slavery. The first battle of Bull Run did away with that idea. The causes *since* for *war* have been as *noble* and *greater far than those that urged our fathers on. Even* should we allow they were wrong at the beginning of this contest, *cruelty and injustice* have made the wrong become the *right*, and they stand *now* (before the wonder and admiration of the world), as a noble band of patriotic heroes. Hereafter, reading of *their deeds*, Thermopylæ will be forgotten.

When I aided in the capture and execution of John Brown, (who was a murderer on our western border, who was fairly *tried* and *convicted*, before an impartial judge and jury, of treason, and who, by the way, has since been made a god), I was proud of my little share in the transaction, for I deemed it my duty, and that I was helping our common country to perform an act of justice. But what was a crime in poor John Brown is now considered (by themselves) as the greatest and only virtue of the whole Republican party. Strange transmigration ! *Vice* is to become a *virtue*, simply because *more* indulge in it.

I thought then, *as now*, that the abolitionists *were the only traitors* in the land, and that the entire party deserved the same fate as poor old Brown, not because they wish to abolish slavery, but on account of the means they have ever endeavored to use to effect that abolition. If Brown were living, I doubt whether he *himself* would set slavery against the Union. Most, or many, in the North, do, and openly curse the Union, if the South are to return and retain a *single right* guaranteed to them by every tie which we once *revered as sacred*. The South can make no choice. It is either extermination or slavery for *themselves* (worse than death) to draw from. I know *my* choice.

I have also studied hard to discover upon what grounds the right of a State to secede has been denied, when our very name, United States, and the Declaration of Independence, *both* provide for secession. But this is no time for words; I write in haste. I know how foolish I shall be deemed for undertaking such a step as this, where, on one side, I have many friends and every thing to make me happy, where my profession *alone* has gained me an income of *more than* twenty thousand dollars a year, and where my great personal ambition in my profession has such a great field for labor. On the other hand, the south have never bestowed upon me one kind word; a place now where I have no friends, except beneath the sod; a place where I must either become a private soldier or a beggar. To give up all of the *former* for the *latter*, besides my mother and sisters, whom I love so dearly (although they so widely differ with me in opinion) seems insane; but God is my judge. I love *justice* more than I do a country that disowns it; more than fame and wealth; more (heaven pardon me if wrong) more than a happy home. I have never been upon a battle field, but O, my country-men, could you all but see the *reality* or effects of this horrid war, as I have seen them in every *State* (save Virginia), I know you would think like me, and would pray the Almighty to create in the northern mind a sense of right and justice (even should it possess no seasoning of mercy), and that he would dry up this sea of blood between us, which is daily growing wider. Alas! poor country, is she to meet her threatened doom? Four years ago I would have given a thousand lives to see her remain (as I had always known her) powerful and unbroken. And even now I would hold my life as nought, to see her what she was. O, my friends! if the fearful scenes of the past four years had neven been enacted, or if what has been had been but a frightful dream from which we could now awake, with what overflowing hearts could we bless our God and pray for his continued favor. How I have loved the *old flag* can never now be known. A few years since and the world could boast of *none* so pure and spotless. But I have of late been seeing and hearing of the *bloody deeds* of which she has *been made the emblem*, and would shudder to think how changed she has grown. O, how I have longed to see her break from the mist of blood and death that circles round her folds, spoiling her beauty and tarnishing her honor. But no: day by day she has been dragged deeper and deeper into cruelty and oppression, till now (in my eyes) her once bright red stripes look like *bloody gashes* on the face of heaven. I look now upon my early admiration of her glories as a dream. My love (as things stand to-day) is for the South alone. Nor do I deem it a dishonor in attempting to make for her a prisoner of this man, to whom she owes so much misery. If success attends me, I go penniless to her side. They say she has found *that* "last ditch" which the North have so long derided, and been endeavoring to force her in, forgetting they are our brothers, and it is impolitic to goad an enemy to madness. Should I reach her in safety and find it true, I will proudly beg permission to triumph or die in that same "ditch" by her side.

A Confederate, doing duty on his own responsibility.

J. Wilkes Booth.

The Murderer Seen.

Sergeant J. M. Dye, Battery C, Pennsylvania Independent Artillery, stationed at Camp Barry, near Washington, in a private letter of the 15th instant, to his father, J. S. Dye, No. 100 Broadway, New York, gives the following account of the conduct of Booth, immediately before the assassination.

Washington, D. C., April 15, 1865.

Dear Father:—With sorrow I pen these lines. The death of President Lincoln has deeply affected me. And why shouldn't it, *when I might have saved his precious life?*

I was standing in front of the theatre when the two assassins were conversing. I heard part of their conversation. It was not sufficiently plain for an outsider to understand the true meaning of it: yet it apprised Sergeant Cooper and myself that they were anxious that the President should come out to his carriage, which was standing just behind us. The second act would soon end, and they expected he would come out then. I stood awhile between them and the carriage, with my revolver ready, for I began to suspect them. The act ended, but the President did not appear; so Booth went into a restaurant and took a drink, then came out and went into an alley where his horse was then standing; though I did not know that any horse was there. He came back and whispered to the other rascal, then stepped into the theatre. There were at this time two police officers standing by them. I was invited by my friend C. to have some oysters, and we went into a saloon around the corner, and had just got seated when a man came running in and said the President was shot! This so startled us that we could hardly realize it, but we stepped out and were convinced.

Yours,   J. M. DYE.

In addition to the foregoing mass of evidence, convicting Booth beyond all possibility of doubt of the monstrous crime associated with his name, had we space, we could support it with an abundance more of equal strength. The assassin will be remembered to have dropped his hat, pistol, and spur in his passage from the bloody box to the stage and across it behind the scenes. The hat and pistol have both been identified as belonging to Booth, also the vagrant spur. This last article was identified by the livery stable man, from whom he obtained it with the horse on the night of the murder. The circumstance, too, about leaving the stable with the horse just before the murder, points to him with irresistible significance.

The Assassin's Weapons.

The murderer's pistol is a Derringer, the barrel about three inches long. In the stock of the pistol were three caps. The pistol is an old-fashioned one, silver mounted, and of French manufacture. A large knife was found on F. street between Eighth and Ninth. The blade of the knife is about seven inches long, and it is a very dangerous looking weapon. It is thought this is the knife which he held in his hand when he jumped from the box, and with which he intended to have murdered General Grant.

Booth's Room.

This fiend is said to have a room at the National Hotel, Washington, at the time of his diabolical crime, known as the room numbered 228. With the exception that letters and several other articles necessary to the conviction of the assassin have been taken from the room, it remains undisturbed. The room is on the fourth story of the hotel, and has a bare and desolate look. On the bureau, in a brown paper, lies half a pound of Killikinick tobacco, a clothes brush, a broken comb, and a pair of embroidered slippers. Scattered among the drawers were one shirt, two pair of drawers, several pairs of stockings, a half bottle of hair oil, and an old programme of the Oxford Concert Room. On the table lay several sheets of note paper, with a number of the hotel envelopes. A pair of black cassimere pantaloons, marked J. Wilkes Booth on the fob pocket, was the only article of clothing remaining. His trunk, which was locked, was marked with his name, and the word "theatre" following the erasure of the name between the two. A large black leather valise sat on the floor near the trunk, and near it a pair of boots unpolished. The general aspect of things in the apartment was one of hasty exit. The articles mentioned are the only ones in the room.

Attempted Assassination of Secretary Seward.

The murderer directly instrumental in seeking the death of Mr. Seward, by plunging a knife at his throat, is a little more involved, as to personal identity, than the assassin of Mr. Lincoln, but he unquestionably was a member of the same fiendish conspiracy. Several arrests have been made of accomplices, while the principal villain himself is believed to be identified beyond scarcely the shadow of a doubt.

Meanwhi.e we subjoin a highly interesting record of Mr. George F. Robinson's evidence, the nurse in attendance upon Secretary Seward on the night of the 14th instant, and through whose brave and determined endeavors the consummation of the murderous designs of the fiend were frustrated. His statement of the attempt to murder the Secretary cannot fail to be read with interest.

Mr. Robinson is a soldier, belonging to Company E, of the 8th Maine Volunteers. On the 11th of August he came to Douglas Hospital badly wounded. After he had partially recovered, he obtained a furlough to return home, and subsequently another furlough, having been almost continually since the 11th of August unfit for military service. He returned to the hospital after his second furlough, on the 4th of last February. On the 12th of April he was detailed to act as nurse for Secretary Seward, and the arrangement was that he was to remain with him from five o'clock in the evening until after breakfast the next morning. He had entirely recovered from the effects of his wound, also from a spell of sickness afterterwards, but had not quite regained his strength.

What Mr. Robinson says.

Mr. Robinson states that on the morning of the 13th instant, while seated at breakfast in the breakfast-room of the Secretary's residence, which room fronts on the street, a person bearing a most remarkable resemblance to, if he was not the same man who subsequently committed the horrible attempted assassination of the Secretary, stopped at the window, and inquired as to the condition of the Secretary's health. Mr. Robinson supposed him to be some friend of the family, and opened the window and answered his question. The next morning, on the 14th, on the night of which the assassination was attempted, the same person again appeared and asked a similar question. No suspicion was excited in the mind of Mr. Robinson, however, and for the reason as above stated, that he considered him a personal friend of the family.

To the best of the recollection of Mr. Robinson, the man entered the room in which Mr. Seward lay about ten o'clock in the evening. His recollection of the time is very distinct, as only a short time previous he had looked at the thermometer to see that the proper temperature of the room was preserved, and at the same moment observed the time by a watch. Mr. Seward was bolstered up, on a long French bedstead, in a reclining posture, and was quietly sleeping. The lights were turned dimly down, and the arrangements had been perfected for the night. Miss Fanny Seward was also in the room at the time. Presently he heard a man's footsteps ascending the stairs with heavy and noisy tread, and Miss Seward and he were both surprised at this. Then there was a pause. It appears that the man was met at the landing by Mr. Frederick Seward, and with whom he had some conversation—probably referring to his alleged mission from the attending physician—for, a short time afterwards, Mr. Seward entered, and noticing that his father slept, said: "Father is asleep now; I guess we will not disturb him." Miss Seward followed her brother to the door, looked out, and returned; and she did this the second time, then returned and sat down on the bedside. As soon as she was seated the second time, a slight noise was heard on the staircase, as though a man had struck another with a walking-cane. Mr. Robinson opened the door slightly to see what was the cause of the disturbance.

The moment Mr. Robinson opened the door, he saw a man who appeared to be covered with blood, whom he supposed to be Major Seward, and immediately in front of him the assassin. The villain was about six feet in height, of medium-sized, round face, of extremely light complexion, with light sandy hair, and whiskers and moustache, both light in color and growth, and was broad-shouldered. He wore a slouched hat, which he left behind, a light-colored overcoat, buttoned closely to the throat with what seemed to be pearl buttons. His hands were soft and delicate-looking, but he displayed wonderful muscular power. As Mr. Robinson opened the door the assassin struck at his breast. In his hand he had a long knife, the blade of which appeared to be about twelve inches in length and one inch in width. Robinson determined to oppose his progress, and raised his arm to parry the blow. The consequence was that a wound was inflicted in the centre of Mr. Robinson's forehead close to the hair, which he wears turned back. The knife glanced, and the clenched hand in which the man held the dagger came down upon Mr. Robinson's face, and felled him to the floor. Miss Seward at this juncture, escaped from the room, and ran to the front window, screaming "murder."

The assassin leaped on to the bed where Mr. Seward lay, still apparently in a helpless condition, and gave a tremendous blow at his face. He missed his mark, however, and, in his effort, almost fell across Mr. Seward's body.

By this time Robinson had recovered, jumped on to the bed, and caught hold of the assassin's arms. While he was thus attempting to hold the assassin, the latter struck Mr. Seward on the left side of the face, and then on the right side.

The assassin then raised up, and he and Robinson came to the floor together. They both got on to their feet, Robinson still keeping a firm hold upon him. The assassin reached his left arm over Robinson's shoulder, and endeavored to force him to the floor. Finding he could not handle Robinson in that position, he drooped his pistol which had been forced against Mr. Robinson's face in the hand which was around his neck, caught hold of Robinson's right arm with his left hand, and struck behind Robinson with his knife.

They still continued to struggle for a few moments, Robinson forcing him toward the door, which was opened with the intention of throwing him over the balusters. When they had nearly reached the door, Major Augustus H. Seward entered the room, Robinson calling upon him to take the knife out of the assassin's hand. Major Seward immediately clutched the assassin. The latter struck Robinson in the stomach, knocking him down, broke away from Major Seward, and rushed down the stairs.

During the scuffle between Robinson and the assassin, when, Mr. Robinson cannot say, he (the latter) received a wound quite serious, some two inches in breadth, on the upper part of the right shoulder blade, another, a slight one, on the left shoulder. While struggling with the man near the bedside, he had seized the wrist of his right hand, in which was the dagger, and did not release his hold until knocked down by the assassin near the door, and after Major Seward had come to his assistance.

He returned to the room after he found that the assassin had escaped, and found that the Secretary had got off the bed on to the floor, dragging with him the bed clothes, and was lying in a pool of blood. Upon going to the Secretary he found no pulse in his wrist, and stated to Miss Seward who had re-entered the room, and asked if her father was dead, that he "believed he was," but upon a second examination, Robinson ascertained that his heart was still beating.

The Secretary then said, "I am not dead. Send for the police and a surgeon, and close the house." He then placed the Secretary upon the bed, telling him that he "must not talk." Mr. Seward did not speak after that.

Mr. Hansell subsequently told Mr. Robinson that, having been alarmed by the noise, he had started for the Secretary's room, and was met on the stairway by the assassin, and was wounded and thrust to one side.

Mr. Robinson remained with Mr. Seward until next morning at eleven o'clock, when he was removed to Douglas Hospital. Every attention is being paid to this brave man by the surgeons of this institution, and his condition is very favorable.

A Coat Found.

Soon after the assassination, a gray coat, stained with blood, and which had evidently been worn as an overcoat, was found near Fort Bunker Hill, just back of Glenwood Cemetery. In the pocket was a false moustache, a pair of riding gloves, and a slip of paper, upon which was written "Mary E. Gardiner, 419." This is supposed to have been worn by the man who attacked Secretary Seward, although the weight of the evidence indicates that all the conspirators took the same route, that of the Navy Yard bridge.

The Surratt Family.

Suspicion having been directed towards a house occupied by members of the Surratt family, on H street, near Sixth, Major Smith, of General Augur's staff, accompanied by a captain and a gentleman connected with the War Department named Morgan, on Monday night of last week visited the premises, and placing the lady inmates under arrest, proceeded to the examination of the house and papers found in it.

While doing so a rap was heard at the door, about 3 o'clock on Tuesday morning, which was opened by Mr. Morgan, revealing a medium-sized man, and apparently in coarse clothes, covered with mud, and having a pickaxe on his shoulder, black cloth pantaloons and fine boots.

Upon discovering the officers he manifested considerable surprise, and remarked that he had got in the wrong house. In reply to the questions of Major Smith, he gave contradictory answers, some of which were quite absurd.

The man claimed to earn a living by the use of his pick, but on removing the mud from his person he turned out to be of much more genteel appearance than his disguise indicated. He stood forth dressed in a gray coat and vest, black cloth pantaloons and fine boots; and the delicate appearance of his hands and his inconsistent statements, convinced the officers that he had some connection with the attempt to assassinate Mr. Seward, and he was at once taken to General Augur's head-quarters.

Upon reaching head-quarters he was placed in the midst of a group of persons, while an officer was despatched to the residence of Secretary Seward for the colored servant who was at the door at the time the assassin applied for admission. The servant had no knowledge of the arrest of the prisoner as the object in sending for him.

Character of Surratt.

This individual at first supposed to have been the ruffian who attempted the life of Secretary Seward, is described as having been for many years a desperado of the worst character. Not long since a suit was brought against him by a young lady residing across Eastern Branch, for seduction, and so desperate was his character that for some time the officers were afraid to serve the writ; but one of them by laying in ambush succeeded in taking him.

Surratt, it is now thought, was not a direct actor in the assassination, but seems to have been in some way accessory.

Rewards for the Capture of the Assassins.

The Secretary of War, over his own official signature, has offered a reward of $50,000 for the arrest of the murderer of Mr. Lincoln. $10,000 had been before offered by General Augur for the arrest of the same villain, making $60,000 by the government for this capture alone. Besides, the corporation of Washington has offered $20,000 for the same capture, the city of Baltimore $10,000 more, the city of Philadelphia $10,000 more, and Governor Curtin has offered an additional $10,000, if the assassin is caught within the limits of Pennsylvania. Here is a hundred and ten thousand dollars for the capture of this single wretch. In addition, the Secretary of War has offered a reward of $25,000 each for the arrest of Atzeroth and Harold, suspected accomplices in the Booth conspiracy. The Secretary further promises liberal rewards for all valuable information tending to ferret out the villains, and threatens with summary and condign punishment all who are found secreting and in any way aiding or abetting the escape of the scoundrels.

Arrest of an Accomplice.

J. D. Reamer, a prominent merchant of Hagerstown, Md., was arrested in that place on Tuesday of last week, and lodged in the Old Capitol, charged as conspirator in the murder of Mr. Lincoln. Reamer, in a private conversation some time since, had foretold the exact day of the President's death, which has since proved true to the letter.

Capture of the Murderous Conspirator G. A. Atzeroth.

G. Andrews Atzeroth, a prominent actor in the great assassination, was arrested on the 19th instant, at the house of his cousin, near Germantown, Md. His arrest was made by troops under General E. B. Tyler, stationed at Monocacy Junction.

On the evening of the 18th instant, a party of scouts of the First Delaware Cavalry, Captain Townsend, returned to camp from a scout, and reported that a suspicious character had been seen in the neighborhood of Germantown, a small village about twenty miles toward Washington from here; and from what they could learn he answered the description of one of the suspicious characters concerned in the assassination of the President and Secretary of State.

Captain Townsend, commanding the Independant Scouts, immediately set to work, and Sergeant Zachariah W. Gemmill, of Company D (Captain Townsend's), First Delaware Cavalry, and six men, were ordered to proceed to the house where it was understood Atzeroth was staying, and arrest him and such other men as might be found on the premises. The scouts under command of Sergeant Gemmell left camp about two o'clock on the morning of the 19th, and marched to Germantown. Upon arriving at the house of Reichter, the cousin of the accused, about half-past three o'clock in the morning, the sergeant disposed of his men about the premises to prevent all chances of escape, and in company with some of his men, knocked at the door for admittance. After some hesitation on the inmates, the door was cautiously opened, and the sergeant pushed his way into the room, where he found Reichter's family in bed upon the floor, and the room presenting a very confused appearance. He stated his business to Reichter, and asked him and his wife if there was such a man as Atzeroth in the house. At first they denied that there was, but upon the sergeant informing them that he was going to search the house, they informed him that a cousin from the lower part of Maryland was up-stairs in bed.

Sergeant Gemmill immediately ascended to one of the rooms above, where he found Atzeroth in bed with two young men, all quietly sleeping. They were immediately aroused, their clothing thrown on, and taken down-stairs, where the Sergeant made sure of his man, and made preparation for leaving with his prize. Before starting, he entered into conversation with Reichter and his wife in reference to Atzeroth, but their stories were too conflicting, and such a mass of falsehoods, that he resolved to wait until daylight, and make search for such other evidence as would throw light upon the matter.

Atzeroth's Antecedents.

Atzeroth is a German by birth, but having come to this country when quite a child, he speaks English with as much fluency as a native. He is about five feet seven or eight inches high, with a well-knit and compact frame, and about twenty-nine years of age. His complexion is dark and swarthy, with black crisp hair and moustache; eyes dark gray, deep set and piercing. His forehead is low, and the general contour of his features stamp him as a man of low character, who would stoop to any action, no matter how vile, for money. During his examination by Lieut. Runkle, he manifested considerable of a "devil-may-care" sort of a spirit, and seemed to look upon himself as competent to deal with all ordinary circumstances.

Atzeroth is reported to have said to one of his friends some weeks since, that he "was poor now, but in a few weeks he would have plenty of gold."

An Infamous Admission.

He found, by questioning several parties whom Atzeroth had visited, that the accused had come from Washington a day or two before, and at the house of one of the gentlemen, while eating dinner, had, upon the subject of the assassination being broached, abruptly stopped eating, and made use of the following language : "If all of them had done their duty, Grant would have been served the same way!" After making diligent search for additional evidence in the neighborhood, the Sergeant hooked up Reichter's buggy, and bringing both Reichter and Atzeroth with him, returned to camp and reported to Captain Townsend. After hearing what the Sergeant had to say, the Captain directed that the prisoners should be taken to the head-quarters of Major Arteman, for examination.

The prisoners were examined separately, and their answers throughout were a mass of absurd contradictions. Reichter's house is situated some twelve miles from Washington, in a very secluded and unfrequented spot, surrounded on all sides by immense groves of pines, and in the midst of a neighborhood which has ever been known to be the hiding-place of guerillas and others who wished to commit depredations upon the surrounding country. The inhabitants of the country are, as a class, generally known to be disloyal, and since the arrest of Atzeroth, have been very reticent, almost refusing to answer any questions that may be put to them in reference to the matter of his conduct while with them.

After the examination the prisoners were manacled, and with a guard under Sergeant Gemmill, were sent to the railroad station to be forwarded to the head-quarters of Gen. E. B. Tyler. While here, some five or six detective officers who had been searching for him, came up and fully identified the accused to be the party they were in search of.

ESCAPE OF BOOTH AFTER THE ASSASSINATION.

ATTEMPTED ASSASSINATION OF MR. SEWARD.

ARREST OF THE VILLAIN WHO DID THE BLOODY WORK.

THE RECOGNITION.

CAPTURE MADE AT THE HOUSE OF SURRATT.

WONDERFUL DISGUISES OF THE CULPRIT.

His Behavior after Arrest.

Washington, April 18.—The demoniacal wretch who attempted the life of Mr. Seward and his son Frederick, was captured this morning at 3 o'clock, by detectives who were watching a house occupied by Surratt.

He was disguised as a laborer. His clothes were covered with mud, and he carried a pickaxe on his shoulder, and was without a hat.

When he was arrested, and upon washing the mud from him, he proved quite a different looking person from which his appearance at first had indicated.

At first the assassin refused to give any name whatever. He then gave three different ones, all of which are fictitious.

He was taken to Mr. Seward's house, and placed in a room with two other strangers, when Mr. Seward's servant boy was brought into the room and the question asked of him—"If the man who assaulted Mr. Seward last Friday night was in the room?"

With a shudder he instantly pointed to the party just arrived, and said—"That is the man." He was also identified instantly by other witnesses of the tragedy, who were brought into the room separately.

Not the slightest doubt is entertained by the officers that the person arrested is the assassin who would have murdered a sick man in his bed, and have slaughtered his whole family in carrying out his fell design.

The bloody miscreant has been imprisoned in a perfectly safe place. One of the names given by the assassin was Payne.

Another Account.

Washington, April 18.—Late last night a man disguised as a laborer, and carrying a pick on his shoulder, approached the house occupied by the family of Surratt, in this city, and was about to enter, when he was arrested, and upon washing the dirt from his face he proved to be a different looking person from what his appearance at first indicated.

He called himself Paine, and exhibited not a little embarrassment. He managed to ask, in an agitated tone, why he was arrested.

The colored servant of Secretary Seward was sent for, when he immediately exclaimed:—"That's the man! I know him by his general appearance and his mouth."

The servant said there could be no mistake. Others in Secretary Seward's house at the time, who probably have a recollection of his appearance, will be afforded an opportunity to-day of recognizing him.

He is believed to be Surratt, who perpetrated the dreadful act at Secretary Seward's house on Friday.

The following is a detailed account of the circumstances under which the man supposed to be Surratt was arrested:

For several days past it had been noticed that a number of suspicious persons were in the habit of going into a certain house in the very heart of the city of Washington, and changing their clothes. Last evening information was received about ten o'clock, by the military authorities, that the house was occupied by Mrs. Surratt, the mother of John H. Surratt, implicated as an accomplice in the

5

recent terrible tragedies, and that the occupants of the house could furnish valuable information in regard to the parties charged with complicity in the murder of the President. Colonel Wells, Provost Marshal, ordered the arrest of these parties. Major H. W. Smith, of General Augur's staff, and Captain Wermerskirch, assistant of Colonel Olcott, special commissioner of the War Department, were charged with the execution of this duty. These officers reached the house about half-past ten o'clock, and arrested Mrs. M. E. Surratt and Miss Anna Surratt, mother and sister of John H. Surratt, and Miss Honora Fitzpatrick and a Miss Holahan. Soon afterwards Mr. R. C. Morgan, assistant of Colonel Olcott, arrived, and proceeded to search the house, examine papers, etc. Abundant evidences were discovered of the deep sympathy of the occupants with the rebel cause, and also of their intimacy and very recent communication with J. Wilkes Booth, the murderer. The ladies arrested were each examined separately, and subsequently sent in charge of officers Rosh and Devoe to General Augur's headquarters for further examination. The information obtained from them was so unsatisfactory and contradictory that the four were finally sent to the Old Capitol prison until they are ready to testify more clearly and consistently.

Just as the ladies were preparing to leave the house, there was a light knock at the front door. It was opened by Major Morgan, Major Smith and Captain Wermerskirch standing by, with their pistols ready to be used if necessary. At the door was a young looking man, about five feet eleven inches in statue, light complexion, with peculiarly large gray eyes, and hair that had evidently been dyed. He wore a gray cassimere coat and vest, fine black cloth pantaloons, and fine boots. His boots and pantaloons were covered with mud almost to the knees, and his whole appearance was that of one who had been lying out in the rain. He had a pickaxe on his shoulder. When the door was opened the visitor exclaimed, "I believe I am mistaken," and turned to go away. He was asked by Mr. Morgan who he wanted to see. He answered, "Mrs. Surratt." Mr. Morgan said, "Mrs. Surratt lives here; she is at home; walk in." He then came in, and was ushered into the parlor, while the ladies under arrest were passed out of the house from a back room where they had been assembled. After being seated in the parlor, the man with the pickaxe was closely interrogated as to his business there at that time of night, twenty minutes after eleven, his occupation, etc. In reply he stated that he was a laboring man, and had been sent for by Mrs. Surratt to dig a gutter, and had called to know what time next morning she wished him to come to work; that he had for some time past been employed on the Baltimore and Ohio Railroad as a laborer, that he was at work on the road on Friday last, and slept that night with the other road hands; that he had no money, and earned his living with his pickaxe. He confusedly attempted to tell where he had slept on Sunday night, and where he had been since Saturday morning; but often contradicted himself and broke down completely in this part of his narrative.

During the investigation he produced a certificate of the oath of allegiance, purporting to have been taken by Lewis Paine, of Fauquier county, Virginia, and claimed that that was his name; but when questioned about it, evidently did not know any thing about the date of the certificate. He asserted frequently that he was a poor man, and could neither read nor write, and earned his living by his daily labor; but his language was that of a man of education, and his feet and hands were small and well shaped, the latter being delicate, white and soft as a woman's, and unstained with any mark of toil. He wore on his head a sort of Scotch skull-cap, which on examination was found to have been made by cutting off the arm of a stockinet shirt, or the leg of drawers of the same material, the top of the cap being formed by tying a string around one of the ends. Upon searching his pockets they were found to contain a comb, hair and tooth brushes, a pot of pomatum, a package of pistol cartridges, a new pocket-compass, and twenty-five dollars in greenbacks. After the preliminary examination he was taken in charge of officers Sampson and Devoe, to General Augur's head-quarters, where, upon further examination, he gave an account of himself quite different from the one previously given. It was evident that he was in disguise, and had been completely taken by surprise in finding the officers at the house where he expected to find a welcome and refuge. The facts disclosed in the examination induced the belief that he was the blood-thirsty villain who had attempted the life of Secretary Seward on Friday night. He was placed in a room with two other strangers. The light was made dim, as nearly as possible, in imitation of the condition of the light in Mr. Seward's room on that eventful night, and the domestics of Mr. Seward were sent for. Upon entering the room the porter, a colored boy about seventeen years of age, threw up his hands with an exclamation of horror, and, pointing to the man, said, "That is the man! I don't want to see him; he did it; I know him by that lip!" The servant had already previously described some peculiarity about the upper lip of the man whom he had admitted to commit the foul and murderous deed. He was subsequently recognized by others as the man who perpetrated the murderous deed at Secretary Seward's, and testimony has been procured, tracing him, step by step, from the time of his separation from Booth until he entered Seward's house. The chain of evidence is complete, and fastens upon him as the perpetrator of the horrid crime which has shocked the whole community. The villain was heavily ironed, and placed in confinement on one of the gunboats. The trail of John Wilkes Booth has also been discovered, and it is expected that he, too, will be in custody before morning. Several other parties are now in confinement, who have been ascertained to be accomplices before the fact in the awful tragedy. The investigations already made reveal a plot well laid, and long and carefully matured for murder and arson, on a scale so grandly diabolical as to be hardly conceivable.

ASSASSINS

and the Great Ones of the World who have fallen by their Hands.

Illustrious actions can be most surely entrusted to the universal remembrance of mankind; but great crimes also take their place in memory, and in history, concentrating, as it were, the history of a whole country in one person.

In the midst of happiness, in a time when our national honor is redeemed, when power and peace were brought together, when we had proudly thrown our old flag to the breeze, and joyous throngs met in the streets, brought together by our universal love of country, with hearts full of joy and gratitude to one who bore his honors so meekly, shrinking even from expressions of gratitude for his signal and patriotic services, the pistol of an assassin rouses "through the corridors of time" the memories of those victims and their assassins of whom history has preserved eternal records.

Assassin did not originally mean any one who committed a crime, but the member of a distinct order, meaning a secret sect of the Ishmaelites founded by Hassan Homairi, who, in their technical phrase, was called the Man of the Mountain. This secret society had the pretension to imitate the Christian order of Knighthood. Probably such also is the pretension of the Knights of the Golden Circle; at any rate their missions were alike, for this association spread terror around it by the hideous and unlooked-for crimes it perpetrated.

All the members vowed implicit obedience to their chief, committing even self-destruction at his command. But before these commands were given, it was the custom of the chiefs to throw the executioners of dark deeds into a state of delirium by the intoxicating influence of hemp, or hashish, just as Booth drank brandy before perpetrating the deed that now overshadows the land.

The members, from the custom of taking hashich, came to be called Hashishin, or Hemp-eaters, which being translated and corrupted became in European languages ASSASSIN, ASSASSINO, and so forth. In all times and ages men have been tempted to crime on the good and great.

Constantine VI.

Irene, Empress consort of Greece, was an ambitious woman, by birth a Roman. By the death of her husband she lost her power, which was of course, vested in his successor and son,, Constantine VI. After a long minority, the Empress finding that all authority would now escape her forever, caused her son's eyes to be put out, and then afterwards had him strangled (a favorite way of taking life in those days). Irene reigned herself prosperously, though at last offending the courtiers around her, she was deposed, and finally died in exile.

William Rufus.

William Rufus, the unworthy son of William the Conqueror, who had been a great man, knowing how to conciliate the conquered, was a great hunter. In order to indulge his favorite pastime, he confiscated all the lands that obstructed his project of forming a vast forest in which the game could accumulate.

Sir Walter Tyrrel, one of those who had suffered by this fancy of the king, watching his opportunity, shot him with an arrow, and escaped immediately to France. William Rufus lies buried in Winchester Cathedral, and the new forest, still retaining its name, is one of the most lovely spots in Hampshire.

Cola di Rienzi.

In the days of Clement VI., Di Rienzi, the son of a tavern-keeper and a washer-woman, imbued with an enthusiasm for the great deeds of antiquity, conceived the project of re-establishing a Roman Republic. This wonderful resolution found followers sufficient to become successful, and Rienzi was elected to the head of the Government, under the title of Tribune.

Great was the enthusiasm created by this return to the classical age. Petrarch was one of its great admirers and supporters. But popular favor is vain and unstable, especially in Italy, and a sedition was excited against him. The mob that had once cheered him, now executed him, and he was killed by an infuriated follower of the people, and his body afterwards pierced in their wild fury with innumerable wounds.

Massaniello.

The people of Naples had long suffered under the oppression of the Spanish Viceroys. The people were ready for revolt, when an affray in market, caused by an insult offered by the Spanish authorities to the wife of Tomaso Aniello, commonly called Massaniello, gave the signal for revolt. Massaniello was a man of courage and native genius. He guided the people with judgment and tact, and succeeded in obtaining all he demanded of the Spanish ruler. He was invested with supreme power. Then, all being accomplished, the wily viceroy set to work to destroy the man whom his fears had exalted. In a banquet to which he invited the young liberator of Naples, he administered a drug which, acting on his brain, made him commit acts of madness which lost him the affection of the people. A conspiracy was the consequence, and in an insurrection Massaniello was assassinated by one of his former companions and friends, Gennaro Annese.

James I., of Scotland,

was a man whose mind and genius were far in advance of the country in which he lived. He meditated many rational reforms for the amelioration of the condition of the people, and so, of course, offended the nobility, who decided on getting rid of him.

Surprising him one evening as he sat in the Castle of Perth, in the midst of the queen and her ladies, after a fierce struggle and several escapes, they barbarously stabbed him, inflicting numerous wounds, and killing him almost in the arms of his wife.

The queen, as well as the ladies in attendance, all tried to save him. Catharine Douglas, one of the maids of honor, on the first alarm, finding that a bolt had been removed from a room through which the murderers were heard approaching, thrust her arm through the large staples, and so retarded the entrance of the assassins, until, by their efforts, her arm was crushed as they burst open the doors.

Richard Cœur de Lion, of England.

This chivalrous man, whose deeds have been the theme of poetry and romance, after a most brilliant career, was treacherously killed by the Viscount de Limoges, in France, whilst parleying with him under the protection of a flag-of-truce.

Henry IV., of France and Navarre.

Henry Quatre was one of the most popular monarchs of France. Brave, worthy, just, generous and brilliant, his character suited exactly with the character of the people he governed. Under his rule they were happy and prosperous, yet no less than twenty-eight times was his life attempted. The last attempt was destined to be successful.

The king had been a Protestant, and was suspected by zealous Catholics of only having joined their Church from policy. This armed fanaticism in the person of Francois Ravaillac, who, watching his opportunity, found means to mortally wound the king with a dagger as he was returning on his way to visit his friend and counsellor, the Count de Sully. Ravaillac died on the wheel, which tore him limb from limb.

If the building mania of the present emperor has not destroyed it, there is still in the Rue de la Fernonese (one of the narrowest and dirtiest in the French capital), an inscription on the house in front of which the deed was committed, commemorating the crime and the catastrophe.

Kouli-Khan.

Kouli-Khan was King of Persia. He had been educated by a European, and possessed great intellect and military talent. He meditated the civilization of Persia, as well as its aggrandizement. One of his favorite projects was the conquest of British India, which he accomplished to a certain extent, reaching and taking Delhi.

But his glory and his progressive ideas in government offended the nobles and those around him, and in 1747 he was stabbed in his tent by his nephew, whilst his body-guard, turning traitors, kept all who would have rescued him from approaching.

Gustavus of Sweden.

The death of this good and brilliant monarch has, through romance and opera, become well known. He was killed at a masked ball by Captain Ankerstroem, formerly an officer in the army. The liberal principles of the king, and a discontented and vain disposition, yearning for distinction, impelled this assassination, for which the perpetrator, one of a secret conspiracy, was first degraded by being flogged and then hanged.

George III.

The life of this monarch, whose qualities and defects were alike inoffensive, was attempted several times. The nearest attempt to success was by Margaret Nicholson. The king was getting into his carriage at the garden entrance of St. James' palace, when a woman advanced and presented a petition. Whilst the king was opening it, she struck at him with a knife. The king warded off the blow, and as she was preparing to strike again, one of the yeomen of the guard seized the assassin.

The king, turning to the anxious crowd, exclaimed in a loud voice :—" I am not hurt," and thus prevented a popular outburst. The woman, when examined, was found to be, or pretended to be insane. She was put into a mad-house for life.

Paul I., of Russia.

Paul had wearied the world by his wild career both at home and abroad; his hatred of England amounted to a monomania. He aimed also at the power of his nobles, which in Russia is almost as great as that of the sovereign.

His death was decided on and executed, not only by his nobles, but his wife and children aided in the deed. He was strangled with a silken scarf, after being dragged from his bed, by Count Whalem.

His sons, Constantine and Alexander, were both in the room, and his wife was with her son Nicholas in the adjoining chamber, awaiting the completion of the crime to which both were privy. This crime, which sounds like the dark ages, was committed as late as the year 1801. Alexander succeeded his father to the throne.

Queen Victoria.

If ever monarch was respected or woman loved by a whole nation, that woman is Victoria, Queen of England. Yet no less than five times has her life been attempted. Four of these attempts were, however, by people desiring notoriety, who could give no reasonable motive for the deed. Two of the criminals were sent to an insane asylum for life, whilst two were transported.

The fifth attempt on the life of the Queen was as she was driving from Buckingham Palace, through the park, seated in her usual carriage, an open barouche, with four houses, two servants, and two outsiders ; the Queen was conversing with Prince Albert, smiling and bowing to all the greetings and salutations she received on her way, when the Prince was seen to throw himself suddenly in front of the Queen, and at the same moment the report of a pistol was heard. The ball passed over the head of the Prince.   Prince Albert, gazing out at the crowd, had suddenly seen the bright barrel of a pistol, on which a ray of the sun was shining, and had understood the purport of the man who held it. Without giving any sign of alarm, he hesitated not an instant to sacrifice his own life for that of the Queen, or rather let us think it was the husband who gave his life to save that of his wife.   The assassin was never taken; but the Prince made great progress in the affections of the English people by the spontaneous proof of his love and devotion to their beloved Queen.

Napoleon I.

In the reign of the great Napoleon, there was, it is said, a special department in the office of the secret police dedicated exclusively to discovering plots against the life of the Emperor, and it is also said that this department was never idle. Three or four plots a day was the common allowance.

The greatest and the nearest to success was the attempt (a royalist attempt) by the infernal machine.   This machine was placed in the way Napoleon was to take going from the Tuileries to the opera.   Every thing, especially the exact time of his arrival on the spot, had been calculated—all calculated, in fact, but the influence of Josephine on his destiny.

She it was who saved him.   Just as they were about to depart, she took it into her little coquettish head that the India shawl she wore was not becoming, and sent for another—consequently a delay of over five minutes.   Whilst the Empress was getting her shawl, the fuses were burning, and the machine exploded three minutes before the imperial carriage got to the spot.   Many persons were killed, but Napoleon was saved, and by Josephine, whom, on his marriage day, he had called the "star" of his destiny.

Napoleon III.

Plots and counterplots are said to occupy the mind of the Minister of Police almost as much as in the time of the first Emperor.   The most important attempt on Napoleon's life is the one in which Orsini and Pierri were the conspirators. It was one planned in the manner of the infernal machine.

It exploded as the Emperor approached the opera; many of the projectiles fell into his carriage, yet he was not wounded, neither was the Empress; and Napoleon III. was looked upon by the people as bearing a charmed life.

Orsini and Pierri were Italian patriots, who had belonged to the Carbonari, with whom Louis Napoleon had himself, in his early days in Italy, been associated.

When he attained to power the Carbonari exacted his aid in the restoration of Italian liberty, which aid he promised.   Not fulfilling his promise sufficiently promptly, Orsini and Pierri believed him a traitor to their cause—hence their vengeance.   They were both executed in 1858, and since their death Napoleon, at Magenta and Solferino, fulfilled his promise to the Carbonari, and has made Italy one of the kingdoms of the earth, under an Italian king—Victor Emmanuel.

ATTEMPTED ASSASSINATIONS IN MODERN TIMES.

(From the Toronto Leader.)

A crime so horrible as assassination is held in detestation and abhorrence by every civilized people.   The savage tribes of America, by whom it is systematically practised, resort to it only to avenge the murder of a relative.   Unless under peculiar circumstances, it carries with it the presumption of cowardice, the exceptions being where the horrid deed is done in public, and the perpetrator places his own life in imminent hazard, either from the fury of the populace or those more regular steps which lead through a judicial process to a felon's death.   The assassin of Mr. Lincoln could hardly hope to escape, though the murderer—in intent, if not in fact—of Mr. Seward had more chance in his favor.   There are not wanting, in recent times, plenty of instances of attempts being made to assassinate royal or other eminent political personages; but they have almost invariably miscarried from one cause or another. The attempts on the life of Napoleon III. are fresh in the public recollection; but though they have been more than once repeated, the Emperor of the French still lives. We are many of us old enough to remember the plot of Fiaschi to murder Louis Phillippe, and to recall the days when the Duke of Wellington found it necessary to secure his windows with thick iron shutters. Not all the virtues of our own Queen and the love which is borne her by her subjects have protected her, at all times, from attempts upon her life. In 1840 a madman shot at the Queen and the Princess Royal; and at another time, a captain of dragoons assaulted her Majesty by horsewhipping her. The successful attempt, in recent times, to assassinate a statesman in the case of Mr. Percival, shot by Bellingham in the lobby of the House of Commons, in 1811. Bellingham acted from a sense of personal injury. A Russian merchant, he attributed his ruin to Percival, and took this means of revenge. At a still later date, within about twenty years, an attempt was made on the life of Sir Robert Peel, and the ball intended for him struck and killed his private Secretary, Mr. Drummond. In 1820 was formed the Cato street conspiracy, with Thistlewood at its head, for the purpose of assassinating the whole British Cabinet, at a dinner to be given at Lord Harrowby's house, in Grosvenor Square. The conspiracy was denounced by government spies, and Thistlewood was executed for the crime. About twenty years before this time, a madman named Hadfield fired from the pit of Drury-Lane Theatre at George III. in his box, and missing his aim, was tried for treason, but not convicted, on account of his irresponsible condition. He was kept in confinement for safety. This was the second attempt on the life of that king, Margaret Nicholson having in 1786, attempted to stab his Majesty with a knife as he was alighting from his carriage near St. James' Palace. The woman was treated as a maniac, and confined in Bethlehem Hospital. All these attempts to assassinate royal and distinguished political personages taken together, were not attended with as much success as the two which were made simultaneously at Washington last Friday night. The success of these attempts is more unusual than the acts themselves. And the reasons for that success are plain. An English King may be fired at, as we have seen, from the pit of a theatre, or an Emperor of the French may encounter an attempt at assassination the moment he passes out of the opera into his carriage; but at Washington an assassin can get immediately behind the Chief Magistrate in his box at the theatre, and make sure of his murderous purpose. Percival was shot in the lobby of the House of Commons, and Sir Robert Peel was shot at in the street; but at Washington the assassin, with a clumsy lie in his mouth, finds ready admission to the sick chamber of a feeble and emaciated minister of State, and strikes blows which he intended to be mortal. This strange facility of access to great political personages having proved fatal, may cause the notions of primitive simplicity which were thought to comport with the character of that Republic, to be revised, and it may henceforth be found necessary to surround the President of the United States with that protection which is accorded to Kings and Emperors in Europe. In this way the manners of the Republican court of Washington may undergo a change. Whatever may have been the motive for the assassination of President Lincoln and the attempt on the life of Secretary Seward, they can but inspire horror in all right-minded persons everywhere. So far as the cause of the South is identified with these acts, it will suffer in the estimation of the world. There is nothing to be gained to any cause by so horrible a crime as assassination, and much to be lost. One of the effects will be, in this case, to exasperate the North against the South, and to cause it to insist on much harder conditions, when the question of final reconciliation comes to be discussed, than it otherwise would have done. There were two parties in the North; one in favor of mild measures, such as foregoing the right of confiscating the property of men who had been in arms against the Washington Government; the other insisting on the hanging of Jefferson Davis whenever he should be caught, and similar measures of extreme severity. The "malignants," as they were not inaptly called, were likely to have been greatly in the minority; but the temper of the North will be exasperated by the assassination of their President and the murderous attack upon Secretary Seward, and mild and merciful councils will be likely to be forgotten in the bad feeling that will once more become predominant. Outside the United States, these assassinations will injure the cause of the South in the estimation of the world, precisely in the proportion that Southerners may be found to have been in the plot or to have approved of the crime after its perpetration. That the death of Mr. Lincoln will alter the war policy of the Northern States cannot be supposed. He was but a representative man; and the large vote he recorded on his re-election shows how much more fully he came up to the Northern standard than General McClellan. The assassins have not learned the great lesson that individuals, in great emergencies, count for very little; that it is the general bent of the national mind, and not the will or the power of an individual, that controls the policy of the nation, in circumstances-similar to those of the United States. The policy of the North, be it right or wrong, will not die with President Lincoln.

BOOTH, THE ASSASSIN.

HE IS TRACED TO HIS HIDING-PLACE—HE REFUSES TO SURRENDER HIMSELF.

THE CAPTURE OF HAROLD.

BOOTH SHOWS FIGHT—THE BARN SET ON FIRE.

Death of the Murderer of Lincoln!

HOW BOOTH WAS DISCOVERED—LOYAL NEGROES GUIDE HIS PURSUERS—HIS BODY AT WASHINGTON.

Full Particulars of the Pursuit and Capture.

OFFICIAL GAZETTE.

Washington, April 27—9 30, A.M.—Major-General Dix, New-York : J. Wilkes Booth and Harold were chased from the swamp in St. Mary's county, Maryland, to Garrett's farm, near Port Royal, on the Rappahannock, by Colonel Baker's force.

The rear of the barn in which they took refuge was fired. Booth, in making his escape, was shot through the head and killed, lingering about three hours, and Harold was captured. Booth's body, and Harold, are now here.

(Signed)   EDWIN M. STANTON,
                        Secretary of War.

[Port Royal, Virginia, near which Booth and Harold were taken, is on the south side of the Rappahannock, about twenty miles below Fredericksburg. The belief heretofore entertained, that Booth, after committing his crime, took refuge in the southern counties of Maryland, with a view to crossing the Potomac into Virginia, is confirmed.]

THE PURSUIT AND DEATH OF BOOTH.

Washington, April 27.—Booth, after assassinating President Lincoln and making a tragic exit from the stage of the theatre, mounted his horse and rode off, accompanied by an accomplice, named Harold, a young Marylander. To avoid suspicion, they separated, meeting at a place called Marlboro.

Booth, in jumping from the box, had fractured one of the small bones of his left leg, just above the ankle, and the limb had swollen during the ride, causing much pain. Harold took him to the house of a Dr. Mudge, where the boot was cut off and the limb bandaged.

The two fugitives remained some days in Maryland, and Harold states that

PRESIDENT LINCOLN'S

FUNERAL CAR.

he saw the cavalry and detectives very near their place of concealment several times.

They were harbored by sympathizers with the rebel cause, and the only persons who have given any information about them are those loyal southerners who are easily distinguished by their dark skins.

Colonel Baker on the track of the Assassins.

Meanwhile Colonel L. C. Baker, Provost Marshal of the War Department, had taken no part in the search made in Maryland for Booth by a large military force, aided by Colonel Olcott and the New York detectives, as he was waiting for some definite information of his whereabouts.

On Monday afternoon he received intelligence that Booth and Harold had probably crossed the Potomac at Swan's point. Those engaged in searching for them did not know that they had crossed. Having consulted maps of Virginia, which he obtained from the office of the Coast Survey, Colonel Baker made up his mind that Booth and Harold must have gone to the vicinity of Port Royal, a quiet village below Fredericksburg on the Rappahannock.

He accordingly wrote to General Hancock, requesting him to detail a commissioned officer and twenty-five cavalrymen to report to any one he might designate. He then gave instructions to two of his detective force Lieutenant Luther B. Baker and E. J. Conger, formerly lieutenant-colonel of the cavalry regiment which Colonel Baker commanded.

The Escort.

which subsequently reported and started off under the orders of Detectives Casker and Conger, belonged to the 16th New York Cavalry, which has for some months been looking after Moseby's guerillas over in Virginia.

The Commander of the Escort.

Lieutenant Edward P. Dougherty, who commanded the escort, was at one time a resident in Boston. When the rebellion broke out he came here as a private in the New York Seventy-first, in which regiment he fought at the first Bull Run. He afterwards enlisted in the Berdan Sharp-Shooters, and was then transferred into the Sixteenth New York Cavalry, where he has so distinguished himself as to secure promotion.

He was especially commended last fall when, on making a reconnoissance near Culpepper Court House with a small force, he encountered Kershaw's Rebel Cavalry Division, but gallantly cut his way out.

Booth's Executioner.

Sergeant Boston Corbett, who shot Booth, is a religious enthusiast, who has made the character of Cromwell his study. He was born in England, is about thirty-three years old, and is by trade a hat finisher.

About seven years since, while in Boston, he experienced religion, and when baptized, assumed the name of the city where he became converted, and since then he has always prayed for Divine instruction before taking any step in life, and he says that he has always been prompted what to do.

He was at one time a prisoner at Andersonville, Georgia, and was one of a party of sixteen who escaped. They were hunted down with bloodhounds, and only himself and one of his companions were brought back alive.

On the Sunday after President Lincoln was assassinated, Sergeant Corbbett obtained leave to attend services at McKentree Chapel here, and there prayed fervently that the assassins might be punished.

How the Assassins were Discovered.

The detectives and their escort went down on a steamboat to Belle Plain, where they landed before day on Monday morning, and struck across for the Rappahannock.

There is a ferry above Port Royal, and the ferryman denies having ferried over any men answering to the descriptions of Booth and Harold. But a colored man looking over Lieutenant Baker's shoulder at a photograph of Booth, which he was showing the ferryman, exclaimed: "I saw that man across the river—he was in a wagon with three other men." The loyal although sable Virginian was right. It appears that Booth and Harold had crossed the Potomac in a canoe, for which they paid three hundred dollars, and were met on the Virginia shore by two Confederate officers with a two-horse wagon. Booth wore a grey suit without any military insignia of rank.

At Port Royal the detectives learned that one of the Confederate officers had a sweetheart at Bowling Green, and had probably gone there. So the party started in pursuit, passing on their way a farm where resided two brothers named William and John Garrett, who have been in the Rebel army, their house being about a quarter of a mile from the road.

After having gone about three miles from the Garretts' house, the party met a loyal Virginan, of dark skin, of course, and from him learned that Booth and Harold were at the Garretts'. "Right about!" was the word, and about three o'clock in the morning the pursuers arrived there.

Statement of the Garretts.

Here let us state what the Garretts say about their visitors who came to their house on Friday or Saturday of last week.

The fugitives were brought in a wagon by two Confederate officers, who spoke of Booth as a wounded Marylander on his way home, and that they wished to leave him there a short time, and would take him away by the 26th.

Booth limped somewhat, and walked on crutches about the place, complaining of his ankle. He and Harold regularly took their meals at the house, and Booth kept up appearances well.

One day at the dinner table, the conversation turned on the assassination of the President, when Booth denounced the assassination in the severest terms, saying that there was no punishment severe enough for the perpetrator. At another time some one said in Booth's presence, that rewards amounting to $200,000, had been offered for Booth, and that he would like to catch him, when Booth replied, "Yes, it would be a good haul, but the amount would doubtless soon be increased to $500,000."

After our cavalry passed towards Bowling Green, Booth and Harold applied to one of the Garretts for two horses, that they might ride to Louisa Court House, but he fearing that the horses would not be returned, refused to let them go. Some words of recrimination passed between Booth and Harold, and the Garretts becoming suspicious that all was not right, urged them to leave. This they refused to do unless they could be supplied with horses; and the Garretts then said that if they remained, they must sleep in the barn. One of the Garretts went to sleep in the corn crib, fearing as he says, that the strangers would steal their horses

Preparations for the Capture.

On returning to the Garretts' house, Lieutenant Baker halted his force, and going in, obtained a reluctant confession from the brother there, where the criminals were. Going out again, Lieutenant Baker aroused his escort, who had nearly all gone to sleep, and took them to the barn, around which he stationed them. He then advanced to the door, and knocking with the butt of his revolver, said, "Booth, we want you." "Here I am," replied the assassin, "who are you, Confederate or Yankee?" Lieutenant Baker informed him who he was, and summoned him to surrender, but met with a defiant refusal.

Quite a parley ensued, Harold at one time expressing a desire to surrender, which Booth rebuked, denouncing him as a coward. Booth could see the party outside, through the cracks of the barn, but they could not see him. He swore that he would never be taken alive, and declared that he could kill at least five men, and then kill himself, should they attempt to break into the barn.

The Barn Fired.

At last, Lieutenant Baker, fearing that the guerillas and the paroled Rebel soldiers, with whom the country swarmed, would come to the rescue, posted the cavalrymen around the barn, and going to one end of it, which was filled with hay, pulled some through a crack and lighted it. The flames ran up the crack to the top of the hay-mow, over which they spread. The inside of the barn was now lighted up.

When Booth first saw the fire he clambered up on the mow, and vainly attempted to extinguish it. He then returned to his position on the floor, between the two doors, with his back against the hay-mow, a revolver in each hand, and a Spencer carbine between his legs.

Harold Surrenders.

Meanwhile, the soldiers had approached the barn, and Harold, dropping his pistol, gave himself up, receiving Booth's malediction as he left the burning barn.

Death of Booth.

Just afterwards the roof over the hay-mow began to crack as if it was falling in, and Booth made a movement. Some of those who were watching him say that he was about to kill himself, while others declare that he was intending to break out and escape. Be this as it may, Sergeant Corbett had a sight at him through a wide crack with his cavalry six-shooter, and pulled trigger. The ball entered about where the President was shot, but passed entirely through Booth's head. The murder has been avenged. "It's all up now," shrieked Booth. "I'm gone," and he staggered towards the door of the barn. Lieutenant Baker received him, and taking him from the blazing barn, laid him on the ground, then sat down and took his head in his lap.

Booth did not deny his crime, and showed no signs of repentance or of humanity, except to ask Lieutenant Dougherty to give a message to his mother. His death was not easy, but at three minutes after seven his spirit passed away into the presence of an avenging God.

Return of the Escort.

Nothing remained for the party to do but to regain their steamboat at Belle Plain.

How Harold was taught to Walk.

They had to bring Booth's body in a cart, and at first Harold had to walk, to which he, as a Maryland gentleman, objected, but after a rope was placed around his neck with a slip noose, and the other end was fastened to a cavalryman's saddle, he started off, taking good care that the rope should not tighten.

The Remains of Booth.

From Belle Plain Lieutenant-Colonel Conger, rode overland to Alexandria, and reported to Colonel Baker yesterday afternoon, at half-past five.

When he left there were some hopes that Booth's wound was not mortal.

Colonel Baker went to Alexandria to meet the steamer, and since then the body of Booth, by direction of the Secretary of War, has remained in his custody.

Surgeon-General Barnes, with an assistant, made an autopsy on the remains this afternoon. Their final disposition is unknown to the public as yet.

Such are the leading events of the escape, pursuit, and arrest of the assassin of President Lincoln, obtained from unquestionable resources.

Of course, every member of the expedition, civil or military, regards himself as the principal agent, and some wonderful stories are told; but what I have stated may be relied upon as correct.

This is, however, but the second act in the great conspiracy, the first act of which cost us our President. Other arrests have been made.

Other arrests are to be made, and in due time the public will learn the extent and the deliberate wickedness of the whole crime. They will also see that much of what has been published about arrests of the party who attacked Secretary Seward and other matters are bosh. Colonel Baker has detected the criminal, and the Secretary of War, who knows the facts better than any one else, gives him the credit.

Appearance of the Body.

Booth's moustache had been cut off apparently with scissors, and his beard allowed to grow, changing his appearance considerably. His hair had been cut somewhat shorter than he usually wore it.

Booth's body, which we have before described, was at once laid out on a bench, and a guard placed over it. The lips of the corpse are tightly compressed, and the blood has settled in the lower part of the face and neck. Otherwise the face is pale, and wears a wild, haggard look, indicating exposure to the elements, and a rough time generally in his skulking flight. His hair is disarranged and dirty, and apparently had not been combed since he took his flight. The head and breast is alone exposed to view, the lower portion of his body, including the hands and feet, being covered with a tarpaulin thrown over it. The shot, which terminated his accursed life, entered on the left side at the back of the neck, a a point, curiously enough, not far distant from that in which his victim, our lamented President, was shot.

A Spencer carbine, which Booth had with him in the barn at the time he was shot by Sergeant Corbett, and a large knife, with blood on it, supposed to be the one which Booth cut Major Rathbun with in the theatre box on the night of the murder of President Lincoln, and which was found on Booth's body, have been brought to the city. The carbine and knife are now in the possession of. Colonel Baker, at his office.

Booth had upon his person some bills of exchange, but only about $175 in Treasury notes.

The bills of exchange, which are for a considerable amount, found on Booth's person, were drawn on banks in Canada in October last. About that time Booth was known to have been in Canada.

It is now thought that Booth's leg was fractured in jumping from the box in Ford's Theatre upon the stage, and not by the falling of his horse while endeavoring to make his escape, as was at first supposed.

The Captured Assassins.

The greatest curiosity is manifested to view the body of the murderer Booth, which yet remains on the gunboat in the stream off the Navy Yard. Thousands of persons visited the yard to-day in hopes of getting a glimpse at the murderer's remains, but none were allowed to enter who were not connected with the yard. The wildest excitement has existed here all day, and regrets are expressed that Booth was not taken alive.

Sergeant Corbett.

It is said that in pulling the trigger upon Booth, he sent up an audible petition for the soul of the criminal.

The pistol used by Corbett was the regular large-sized cavalry pistol. He was offered a thousand dollars this morning for the weapon with its five undischarged loads.

An Autopsy.

This afternoon, Surgeon-General Barnes, with an assistant, held an autopsy on the body of Booth.

Booth not in Rebel Uniform.

It now appears that Booth and Harold had on clothing which was originally of some other color than the Confederate gray, but being faded and dusty, presented that appearance.

Booth's Mistress.

The news of Booth's death reached the ears of his mistress while she was in a street car, which caused her to weep bitterly, and drawing a photograph likeness of the murderer from her pocket, kissed it fondly several times.

The Demeanor of Harold.

Harold, thus far, has evaded every effort to be drawn into conversation by those who have necessarily come in contact with him since his capture, but his outward appearance indicates that he begins to realize the position in which he is placed, and that there is no escape from the awful doom that certainly awaits him. His relations and friends, in this city, are in the greatest distress over the disgrace that he has brought upon himself.

Bowling Green.

Bowling Green, near which place Booth was killed, is a post village, the capital of Caroline county, Virginia, on the road from Richmond to Fredericksburg, forty-five miles north of the former, and is situated in a fertile and healthy region. It contains two churches, three stores, two mills and about three hundred inhabitants.

TREATMENT OF TRAITORS.
MARYLAND.
Excitement at Westminster, Md.

On Saturday, on the reception of the intelligence at Westminster, Carroll county, Md., of the assassination of President Lincoln, the most intense excitement ensued. A meeting of the citizens was called at the Court House at eight o'clock P. M., which was presided over by Mr. Shriver, and was the largest and most respectable in point of numbers ever held in the town. Great bitterness of feeling was expressed against Joseph Shaw, the proprietor of the Westminster *Democrat*, a paper in the interest of the rebellion, on account of remarks made in its issue of last week. The editor said, among other things, "Some people hope that Lincoln's life will be spared now, in order that the country may be saved the disgrace of an 'incoherent' Vice-President. But is there not a slight chance of improvement in case that Providence should will it otherwise?" The article continued at length in vituperative language against both the President and Vice-President, such as the rebel sympathizers have so frequently indulged in. A proposition was made in the meeting to destroy the office of the paper, but more moderate counsels prevailed, and the resolution was modified to the effect that Shaw be notified that the *Democrat* would not longer be permitted to be issued in that town. A resolution was also unanimously adopted, by a rising vote of those present, requiring the chairman of the meeting to appoint a vigilance committee for Carroll county, whose duty it should be to take such measures as would prevent the return of any rebel who had ever borne arms against the Government of the United States to that county, no matter whether paroled by Gen. Grant or any other authority. Every person who has ever been in the rebel army will be forced to take up his residence elsewhere, their presence being considered dangerous to the peace of the community. At midnight, long after the meeting adjourned, the office of the *Democrat* was visited, the types, cases, printing paper, in fact all the material, were taken to the street and burned, and the press, stove, etc., in the building broken with axes, crowbars, etc. Though the establishment was completely gutted, the building itself was unharmed.

Later—A Disloyal Editor Killed by Citizens.

Joseph Shaw, editor of the Westminster (Carroll county) *Democrat*, whose paper was mobbed and material destroyed the night after the murder of the President, on account of the disloyal sentiments expressed by the editor, and who was also warned away by the people, returned yesterday to Westminster. Last night he was again waited upon by a delegation of citizens, who knocked at his door. He appeared and fired into the crowd, wounding a young man named Henry Bell. Upon this the enraged citizens killed Shaw on the spot.

MAINE.
Arrests for using Offensive Language.

Two women on the train from Skowhegan, expressed themselves in an offensive manner, exulting over the deed of murder. On their arrival in this city, they were quietly delivered over to a squad of soldiers sent by Colonel Little, at the request of the conductor, and lodged in jail. Several men have been arrested here for like hard language, and placed in confinement. One would have fared bad at the hands of the soldiers, but for the interposition of the police.

NEW YORK.
Scenes in Poughkeepsie.

Intense excitement prevailed here in relation to the national disaster. A woman named Frisbee exulted in public over the assassination of the President, when the house, in Main street, in which she resided, was immediately surrounded by several hundred infuriated people, who demanded her immediate arrest. A young man named Denton interfered with the mob, when he was immediately throttled, and, together with the woman, was handed over to the authorities, who lodged them in jail. This being accomplished, the populace quietly dispersed. The city is draped in mourning, and the gloom is general.

A large crowd of people are passing up Main street, escorting a well-known rebel sympathizer, whom they are compelling to carry the American flag. Stopping in front of the Eastman College, they compelled him to give three cheers for a flag which floated at half-mast over it. No violence was used, but the mob seemed determined.

SARATOGA.

At Saratoga, Rev. Dr. Beecher expelled from his seminary a young lady pupil for remarking that the murder of Lincoln made Saturday the happiest day of her life. The Doctor says that no person with such sentiments shall sleep under his roof.

A workman named Neil was expelled from the arsenal on Saturday, for rejoicing. The other employeés "hustled him out."

MASSACHUSETTS.
A Railroad Superintendent in Difficulty.

A scene occurred to-day in our city, evincing the deep feeling of our entire population in the sad affliction. At an early hour in the forenoon, it was reported that Otis Wright, Superintendent of the Lowell Horse Railroad, had made remarks expressing his gratification at the President's death. The report soon spread over the city, and by nine o'clock a large crowd gathered in front of the Museum Building (the office of the company), demanding that Mr. Wright be given up to them. The Mayor and several policemen were soon on the ground, using their efforts to keep back the crowd, which was attempting to rush up-stairs. Finally the Mayor came out upon the awning and stated that Mr. Wright would make an explanation, the latter making his appearance with an American flag in his hand. The crowd refused to hear him at first, but finally the Mayor secured for him a hearing, when Mr. Wright denied that he had made the statement atrributed to him. This did not satisfy. A gentleman came forward and stated that Mr. Wright said to him, when informed of the President's death, "Who's fool enough to kill the damned old fool?" The crowd then gave Mr. Wright half an hour to leave the city, and ere that time he was on his way to the New Hampshire line.

Traitor Mobbed at Swampscott.

On reception of the news, one George Stone, of Swampscott, said in public, it was the best news we had received for four years, and gave three cheers. The citizens and soldiers of Swampscott took him by force and tarred and feathered him, dragged him through the town in a boat, compelling him to hold the American flag over his head, and upon promising to buy an American flag and keep it up during the mourning for the President, at half-mast, he was set at liberty.

BOSTON.
Weymouth after the Copperheads.

On Saturday evening last, a body of men waited upon Elijah Arnold, of East Braintree, at his home, forced him to come out, make a speech, wave the American flag, and give three cheers for the Union. He had uttered treasonable sentiments, and was compelled to retract them.

An Indignant Congregation.

The pulpit of the Baptist Church in a neighboring town, was supplied yesterday by a stranger, who, in all his introductory exercises and sermon, never deigned even to mention our national calamity in the death of our good President. Immediately after the close of the exercises, a resolution was passed by the congregation, pointedly condemning his course, and giving him fifteen minutes to leave town. He left instanter. This was in Medway village, and the party was Rev. Mr. Massey, of Bellingham, who preached there by exchange.

MOBBING A REBEL SYMPATHIZER IN FALL RIVER — HIS STORE CLEANED OUT — OTHER OBNOXIOUS PERSONS VISITED.

On receipt of the melancholy news of the assassination of the President, and while a large crowd of citizens were gathered around the bulletin-boards reading the despatches and giving expression to their deep and most heart-felt sorrow, a notorious copperhead secesh-sympathizer, and liquor dealer, named Leonard Wood, was heard to declare that it was the best news he had heard for forty years. He had no sooner uttered this atrocious sentiment, than he was seized by the indignant bystanders, struck, booted about the streets, and compelled to go into a store to procure an American flag, unfurl, and salute it with three cheers. He then marched to his store, where he locked himself in; but the crowd surrounded his place, and were making preparations to break in, when the Mayor and City Marshal appeared and escorted him to the lock-up, where he is now confined. The crowd then returned to his store, stove in the windows, and smashed things generally. They then visited other copperheads, compelling them to show the American flag.

OHIO.
Cleveland.

It seems providentially provided for that some villains are fools—so great fools that they parade their villainy before the world. Such was the case of certain traitors in Cleveland on Saturday, who were crazy enough to express their joy at the murder of the President, and received therefor some very rough treatment —no more, however, than their just deserts.

The case of J. J. Husband, the well-known architect, who occupies an office and rooms over Fogg's store, was most prominent. He was in high glee over the news, remarking to one man, "You have had your day of rejoicing, now I have mine !" to another, "This is a good day for me !" and to a third, that "Lincoln's death was a d—d small loss !" It seems that afterwards he became sensible of the danger he had incurred by these remarks, for he came sneaking to the newspaper offices to deny that he had made them. We have, however, the authority of half a dozen reliable gentlemen, who heard his remarks, against his unsupported assertion. On his way back to his office he was assaulted by the crowd, but escaped from them. His words were repeated from mouth to mouth, and the indignation of the multitude knew no bounds. The crowd searched the building for him, at last finding him on the roof of the building— He was caught, thrown through the sky-light into his room, and knocked and kicked down-stairs. The mob then set upon him, and would perhaps have pounded him to death had he not been rescued by prominent citizens. He was taken to the court-house and locked up in a room for safe-keeping. He broke out and sneaked off during the day, and, we understand, has since left town. He can never show his face again in Cleveland. His name has already been chipped from the place on the court-house where it was cut as the architect.

Another man, named James Griffith, from Hamilton, Butler county, in this State, arrived in town Saturday morning, and, on hearing of the news, said to a barber who was shaving him in the Weddell House barber-shop, that "Lincoln was a d—d son of a b—h, and ought to have been shot long ago !" Hearing of this the mob started after him. He was taken charge of by Clark Warren and others, who carried him to the jail. On the way there, however, the mob got at him and pounded him badly. He is now in jail, and ought to stay there for a term of months.

Another traitor, expressing his joy on Ontario street, Saturday morning, was knocked stiff by a little fellow half his size. Other men of southern sympathies knew enough to keep closely at home Saturday. Cleveland is an unhealthy place for rebels.

CALIFORNIA.
Onslaught on the Newspaper Offices.

The news of President Lincoln's assassination created the most intense and universal feeling ever witnessed on this coast. It is known already throughout the State, wherever the telegraph extends, and everywhere public demonstrations of grief and horror prevail. Business has been entirely suspended here, the bells are tolling and private buildings are draped in mourning. The authorities thought it prudent to take precautions against popular tumults resulting from expressions of joy by secessionists. Several treasonable brawlers were saved from being lynched by the police. A mob has just entered the publication offices of the *Democratic Press*, *News Letter*, *Monitor* and *Occidental*, copperhead organs, and emptied their contents into the street, amid the applause of an immense crowd. A large body of armed police were ordered out to disperse the mob, but arrived too late to prevent these acts of violence. Other democratic newspaper offices are threatened.

Treatment of a Taitor at Harrisburg.

When the news reached here of the assassination of the President, a man on the street gloried in the fact, and made a most obscene remark in regard to the corpse. The people desired to treat the man in a summary manner, but a guard of soldiers took possession of him. This afternoon he was marched through the principal streets to the tune of the Rogue's March, holding in his hand a board with this inscription : "William Young, a traitor too cowardly to fight for the Rebels, ejects his vulgar venom by insulting the remains of our dead President."

The soldiers desired to ride him on a rail, but the officers would not allow it.

On being released he was followed by a large crowd, yelling and hooting at him, treating him rather roughly.

PHILADELPHIA.
Carrying Concealed Deadly Weapons.

Edward Ingersoll, who resides near Germantown, was arrested yesterday morning by officer John Jones, on the charge of carrying a concealed deadly weapon, and committing an assault and battery on Captain J. B. Withington, Jr., still suffering from a wound received in battle. It seems that the defendant entered a car on the 9 o'clock train from Germantown, at Tioga station. A number of persons called him a traitor, and as he passed into the smoking car, several gentlemen remarking that the presence of a traitor was offensive, he left that car. The train finally reached the depot, and defendant alighted at Ninth and Wallace streets. Captain Withington, of the 198th Regiment Pennsylvania Volunteers, stepped forward, and, addressing defendant, said, "You ought to apologize for your remark made in your speech, that the Southerners were chivalric and noble, and were fighting against an odious tyranny." It is alleged that defendant said, "Go to h—l." Capt. W. raised his cane, but being an invalid could not use it with alacrity. He made a blow at defendant with it, and the latter warded it off with his cane, which was broken by the force of the blow. Instantly defendant presented a revolver, and in a moment the crowd closed in upon him. Officer Jones, who at the same moment was attracted to the spot, took Ingersoll into custody, and conducted him to the lockup at Spring Garden Hall. The magistrate was sent for, and the hearing progressed, at the conclusion of which he asked the defendant if he had any thing to say, or questions to ask. Defendant replied that he pulled the pistol out and cocked it, and the crowd ran like sheep.

Some one said, "You are a liar," and the entire body of spectators made a surge towards him, but nobody was hurt. The defendant was committed in default to answer the charge as preferred against him. He had only received a slight scratch on his face, from a splinter of his own cane. He was taken to the county prison yesterday afternoon. A writ of habeas corpus will probably be taken out, made returnable to-morrow.

This fellow has made himself publicly and personally odious, by his treasonable speeches, ever since the rebellion broke out.

Another Scene.

While Edward was in the lockup at Spring Garden Hall, he was visited by his brother Charles. Upon retiring, some one in the crowd struck him. Charles hastened to his carriage, and just as he got in he received a slight blow on the head. The driver put the whip to the horses, and off they dashed at a fast speed. There was considerable excitement during these proceedings, which increased as the crowd augmented, but there was no general outbreak. We understand that a young man quietly procured a rope that had a slip-knot already made in the middle. This was intended to be placed over the head of Ingersoll, in which event he would probably be strangled to death. His arrest, in all probability, saved his life, as nobody seemed desirous to interfere with him while he was in the custody of the law officers.

www.ingramcontent.com/pod-product-compliance
Lightning Source LLC
Chambersburg PA
CBHW031452270326
41930CB00007B/968